Cambridge
Key English Test for Schools
1

WITH ANSWERS

Examination papers from
University of Cambridge
ESOL Examinatio

CAMBRIDGE
UNIVERSITY PRESS

CAMBRIDGE
UNIVERSITY PRESS

University Printing House, Cambridge CB2 8BS, United Kingdom

One Liberty Plaza, 20th Floor, New York, NY 10006, USA

477 Williamstown Road, Port Melbourne, VIC 3207, Australia

4843/24, 2nd Floor, Ansari Road, Daryaganj, Delhi – 110002, India

79 Anson Road, #06–04/06, Singapore 079906

Cambridge University Press is part of the University of Cambridge.

It furthers the University's mission by disseminating knowledge in the pursuit of education, learning and research at the highest international levels of excellence.

www.cambridge.org
Information on this title: www.cambridge.org/9780521139922

First published 2010
Reprinted 2017

Printed in Italy by Rotolito Lombarda S.p.A.

A catalogue record for this publication is available from the British Library

ISBN 978-0-521-17682-8 Student's Book without answers
ISBN 978-0-521-13992-2 Student's Book with answers
ISBN 978-0-521-14569-5 Audio CD
ISBN 978-0-521-17833-4 Self-study Pack

Contents

Acknowledgements

A guide to KET for Schools   5

Test 1   Paper 1   14
                    Paper 2   26
                    Paper 3   33

Test 2   Paper 1   34
                    Paper 2   46
                    Paper 3   53

Test 3   Paper 1   54
                    Paper 2   66
                    Paper 3   73

Test 4   Paper 1   74
                    Paper 2   86
                    Paper 3   93

Visual materials for Paper 3   94

Paper 3 frames Test 1   102
                    Test 2   105
                    Test 3   108
                    Test 4   111

Test 1   Key   114
Test 2   Key   122
Test 3   Key   130
Test 4   Key   138

Sample answer sheets   146

Acknowledgements

The publishers are grateful for permission to reproduce copyright material. It has not always been possible to identify the sources of the material used, and in such cases the publishers would welcome information from the copyright owners.

Getty Images for p 18/Martin Ruegner; Photolibrary.com for pp 15/Oliver Gutfleisch, 38/Ryan Smith/Somos Images, 78/Gerhard Zwerger-Schoner; Shutterstock for pp 20/Julien Tromeur, 35/muzsy, 40/Yulia Popkova, 55/Charlie Hutton, 58/Timothy Large, 60/Maria Simonova, 75/Christopher Futcher, 80/muzsy.

Picture research by Kevin Brown

Book design by Peter Ducker MSTD

Publishing management by hyphen

The CD which accompanies this book was recorded at dsound, London.

A guide to KET for Schools

The KET for Schools examination is part of a group of general English examinations developed by Cambridge ESOL. All five examinations in this suite have similar characteristics but are designed for different levels of English language ability. Within the five levels, KET is at level A2 (Waystage) in the *Council of Europe's Common European Framework of Reference for Languages: Learning, teaching, assessment.*

Examination	Council of Europe Framework Level	UK National Qualifications Framework Level
CPE Certificate of Proficiency in English	C2	3
CAE Certificate in Advanced English	C1	2
FCE First Certificate in English	B2	1
PET for Schools Preliminary English Test	B1	Entry 3
KET for Schools Key English Test	A2	Entry 2

KET for Schools is a popular exam with candidates who are learning English out of personal interest and for those studying English as part of their school studies. It is also useful preparation for higher level exams, such as PET or PET for Schools and other Cambridge ESOL examinations. KET for Schools is an excellent first step, helping you to build your confidence in English and measure your progress. If you can deal with everyday basic written and spoken communication (for example: read simple texts, understand signs and notices, write simple notes and emails), then this is the appropriate exam for you.

There are two versions of KET available: KET and KET for Schools. KET for Schools was introduced to meet the needs of the increasing number of younger candidates taking KET. Both KET and KET for Schools follow exactly the same format and the task types, testing focuses and level of the question papers are identical. The only difference in the two versions of the exams is that the content and treatment of topics in KET for Schools are particularly targeted at the interests and experiences of younger people.

Topics

These are the topics used in the KET for Schools exam:

Clothes	Language	Shopping
Daily life	People	Social interaction
Entertainment and media	Personal feelings, opinions and experiences	Sport
Food and drink	Personal identification	The natural world
Health, medicine and exercise	Places and buildings	Transport
Hobbies and leisure	Schools and study	Travel and holidays
House and home	Services	Weather

KET for Schools content: an overview

Paper	Name	Timing	Content	Test Focus
Paper 1	Reading/ Writing	1 hour 10 minutes	Nine parts: Five parts (Parts 1–5) test a range of reading skills with a variety of texts, ranging from very short notices to longer continuous texts. Parts 6–9 concentrate on testing basic writing skills.	Assessment of candidates' ability to understand the meaning of written English at word, phrase, sentence, paragraph and whole text level. Assessment of candidates' ability to produce simple written English, ranging from one-word answers to short pieces of continuous text.
Paper 2	Listening	30 minutes (including 8 minutes transfer time)	Five parts ranging from short exchanges to longer dialogues and monologues.	Assessment of candidates' ability to understand dialogues and monologues in both informal and neutral settings on a range of everyday topics.
Paper 3	Speaking	8–10 minutes per pair of candidates	Two parts: In Part 1, candidates interact with an examiner; in Part 2 they interact with another candidate.	Assessment of candidates' ability to answer and ask questions about themselves and about factual non-personal information.

Paper 1: Reading and Writing

Preparing for the Reading section

To prepare for the Reading section, you should read the type of English used in everyday life; for example, short magazine articles, advertisements, instructions, etc. It is also a good idea to practise reading short messages, including notes, emails and cards. Remember, you won't always need to understand every word to be able to do a task in the exam.

Before the exam, think about the time you need to do each part and check you know how to record your answers on the answer sheet (see page 146).

Marks

Each item carries one mark, except for question 56 (Part 9), which is marked out of 5. This paper represents 50% of the total marks for the whole examination.

Reading			
Part	**Task Type and Format**	**Task Focus**	**Number of questions**
1	Matching. Matching 5 prompt sentences to 8 notices, plus one example.	Gist understanding of real-world notices. Reading for main message.	5
2	Three-option multiple-choice sentences. Five sentences (plus an integrated example) with connecting link of topic or story line.	Lexical. Reading and identifying appropriate vocabulary.	5
3	Three-option multiple-choice. Five discrete three-option multiple-choice items (plus an example) focusing on verbal exchange patterns. **AND** Matching. Five matching items (plus an integrated example) in a continuous dialogue, selecting from eight possible responses.	Functional language. Reading and identifying appropriate response.	10
4	Right/Wrong/Doesn't say **OR** three-option multiple-choice. One long text or three short texts adapted from authentic newspaper and magazine articles. Seven three-option multiple-choice items or seven Right/Wrong/Doesn't say items, plus an integrated example.	Reading for detailed understanding and main idea(s).	7
5	Multiple-choice cloze. A text adapted from an original source, for example, encyclopaedia entries, newspaper and magazine articles. Eight three-option multiple-choice items, plus an integrated example.	Reading and identifying appropriate structural word (auxiliary verbs, modal verbs, determiners, pronouns, prepositions, conjunctions, etc.).	8

Preparing for the Writing section

To prepare for the Writing section, you should take the opportunity to write short messages in real-life situations, for example, to your teacher or to other students. These can include invitations, apologies for missing a class, notices about lost property, etc. They can be handwritten or sent as an email.

Before the exam, think about the time you need to do each part and check you know how to record your answers on the answer sheet (see page 147).

Writing			
Part	**Task Type and Format**	**Task Focus**	**Number of questions**
6	Word completion. Five dictionary definition type sentences (plus one integrated example). Five words to identify and spell.	Reading and identifying appropriate lexical item, and spelling.	5
7	Open cloze. Text of type candidates could be expected to write, for example, a short letter or email. Ten spaces to fill with one word (plus an integrated example) which must be spelled correctly.	Reading and identifying appropriate word with focus on structure and/or lexis.	10
8	Information transfer. Two short authentic texts (emails, adverts, etc.) to prompt completion of an output text (form, note, etc.). Five spaces to fill on output text with one or more words or numbers (plus an integrated example).	Reading and writing down appropriate words or numbers with focus on content and accuracy.	5
9	Guided writing. Either a short input text or rubric to prompt a written response. Three messages to communicate in writing.	Writing a short message, note or postcard of 25-35 words.	1

Part 6

This part is about vocabulary. You have to produce words and spell them correctly. The words will all be linked to the same topic, for example, food. You have to read a definition for each one and complete the word. The first letter is given to help you.

Part 7

This part is about grammar and vocabulary. You have to complete a short gapped text of the type you could be expected to write, for example, a note and a reply, or a short letter. You must spell all the missing words correctly.

Part 8

This part tests both reading and writing. You have to use the information in one or two short texts, for example, a note, email or advertisement, to complete a document such as a form, notice, diary entry, etc. You will need to understand the vocabulary used on forms, for example, surname, date of birth, etc. You will need to write only words or phrases in your answers, but you must spell these correctly.

Part 9

You have to write a short message (25–35 words). You are told who you are writing to and why, and you must include three content points. To gain top marks, all three points must be included in your answer, so it is important to read the question carefully and plan what you are going to write. Before the exam, practise writing answers of the correct length. You will lose marks for writing fewer than 25 words, and it is not a good idea to write answers that are too long.

Mark Scheme for Writing Part 9

There are five marks for Part 9. Minor grammatical and spelling mistakes are acceptable but to get five marks you must write a clear message and include all three content points.

Mark	Criteria	
5	All three parts of message clearly communicated. Only minor spelling errors or occasional grammatical errors.	
4	All three parts of message communicated. Some non-impeding errors in spelling and grammar or some awkwardness of expression.	
3	All three parts of message attempted. Expression requires interpretation by the reader and contains impeding errors in spelling and grammar.	Two parts of message are clearly communicated. Only minor spelling errors or occasional grammatical errors.
2	Only two parts of message communicated. Some errors in spelling and grammar. The errors in expression may require patience and interpretation by the reader and impede communication.	
1	Only one part of message communicated. Some attempt to address the task but response is very unclear.	
0	Question not attempted, or totally incomprehensible response.	

Paper 2: Listening

Paper format
This paper contains 5 parts.

Number of questions
25

Task types
Matching, multiple-choice, gap-fill.

Sources
All texts are based on authentic situations, and each part is heard twice.

Answering
Candidates indicate answers either by shading lozenges (Parts 1–3) or writing answers (Parts 4 and 5) on an answer sheet.

Timing
About 30 minutes, including 8 minutes to transfer answers.

Marks
Each item carries one mark. This gives a total of 25 marks, which represents 25% of the total marks for the whole examination.

Preparing for the Listening test
The best preparation for the Listening test is to listen to authentic spoken English for your level. Apart from understanding spoken English in class, other sources include: films, TV, DVDs, songs, the internet, English clubs, and other speakers of English, such as tourists, guides, friends and family.

You will hear the instructions for each task on the recording and see them on the exam paper. There are pauses in the recording to give you time to look at the questions and to write your answers. You should write your answers on the question paper as you listen. You will have eight minutes at the end of the test to transfer your answers to the answer sheet (see page 148). Make sure you know how to do this and that you check your answers carefully.

Part	Task Type and Format	Task Focus	Number of questions
1	Three-option multiple-choice. Short neutral or informal dialogues. Five discrete three-option multiple-choice items with visuals, plus one example.	Listening to identify key information (times, prices, days of week, numbers, etc.).	5
2	Matching. Longer informal dialogue. Five items (plus one integrated example) and eight options.	Listening to identify key information.	5
3	Three-option multiple-choice. Longer informal or neutral dialogue. Five three-option multiple-choice items (plus an integrated example).	Taking the 'role' of one of the speakers and listening to identify key information.	5
4	Gap-fill. Longer neutral or informal dialogue. Five gaps to fill with one or more words or numbers, plus an integrated example. Recognisable spelling is accepted, except with very high frequency words, e.g. 'bus', 'red'; or if spelling is dictated.	Listening and writing down information (including spelling of names, places, etc., as dictated on recording).	5
5	Gap-fill. Longer neutral or informal monologue. Five gaps to fill with one or more words or numbers, plus an integrated example. Recognisable spelling is accepted, except with very high frequency words, e.g. 'bus', 'red'; or if spelling is dictated.	Listening and writing down information (including spelling of names, places, etc., as dictated on recording).	5

Paper 3: Speaking

Paper format
The paper contains two parts. The standard format for Paper 3 is two candidates and two examiners. One examiner acts as an assessor and does not join in the conversation. The other is called an interlocutor and manages the interaction by asking questions and setting up the tasks (see Paper 3 frames on pages 102–113).

Task types
Short exchanges with the examiner and an interactive task involving both candidates.

Timing
8–10 minutes per pair of candidates.

Marks
Candidates are assessed on their performance throughout the test. There are a total of 25 marks in Paper 3, making up 25% of the total score for the whole examination.

Preparing for the Speaking Test
Take every opportunity to practise your English with as many people as possible. Asking and answering questions in simple role plays provides useful practice. These role plays should focus on everyday language and situations and involve questions about daily activities and familiar experiences. It is also a good idea to practise exchanging information in role plays about things such as costs and opening times of, for example, a local sports centre.

Part	Task Type and Format	Length of Parts	Task Focus
1	Each candidate interacts with the interlocutor. The interlocutor asks the candidates questions. The interlocutor follows an interlocutor frame to guide the conversation, ensure standardisation and control level of input.	5–6 minutes	Language normally associated with meeting people for the first time, giving information of a factual personal kind. Bio-data type questions to respond to.
2	Candidates interact with each other. The interlocutor sets up the activity using a standardised rubric. Candidates ask and answer questions using prompt material.	3–4 minutes	Factual information of a non-personal kind, related to daily life.

Assessment

You are assessed on your own individual performance and not in relation to the other candidate. Both examiners assess you – the assessor awards marks according to: Grammar and Vocabulary, Pronunciation and Interactive Communication. The interlocutor awards a mark for overall performance.

Grammar and Vocabulary

This refers to your ability to use vocabulary, structure and paraphrase strategies to convey meaning.

Pronunciation

This refers to the intelligibility of your speech. Having an accent from your first language is not penalised if it does not affect communication.

Interactive communication

This refers to your ability to take part in the interaction appropriately. Hesitation while you search for language is expected and not penalised so long as it does not strain the patience of the listener. You are given credit for being able to ask for repetition or clarification if necessary.

Global achievement

This is based on the analytical criteria and relates to your performance overall.

Further information

The information in this practice book is designed to give an overview of KET for Schools. For a full description of all of the Cambridge ESOL exams, including information about task types, testing focus and preparation, please see the relevant handbooks which can be obtained from Cambridge ESOL at the address below or from the website: www.CambridgeESOL.org

University of Cambridge ESOL Examinations
1 Hills Road
Cambridge CB1 2EU
United Kingdom
Telephone: +44 1223 553355
Fax: +44 1223 460278
Email: ESOLHelpdesk@CambridgeESOL.org

Test 1

PAPER 1   READING AND WRITING (1 hour 10 minutes)

PART 1

QUESTIONS 1–5

Which notice **(A–H)** says this **(1–5)**?

For questions **1–5**, mark the correct letter **A–H** on your answer sheet.

Example:

0 The time of this has changed.   *Answer:*

0	A	B	C	D	E	F	G	H
	☐	☐	☐	☐	☐	■	☐	☐

---

1 You are told if your favourite team has won.

A
> **HOBBS SPORTS SHOP**
> **SALE**
> Starts next week

B
> **Sports Centre**
> Boys' Changing Room
> (for dry sports only)

2 Come on this day and find out why sport is good for you.

C
> 24-hour football information line
> 01894275
> All calls 5p per minute

3 You can watch a sports competition here this afternoon.

D
> Volleyball team
> Players needed - Learn more 7 p.m. tonight
> Sports Hall

E
> **Talk by school visitor**
> Play sport and stay fit
> 4 p.m. March 15th

4 If you like this sport, go to the meeting this evening.

F
> Earlier start for tomorrow's
> football practice
> 9 a.m.

G
> **EASTON SCHOOL**
> No football matches this afternoon
> Grass too wet

5 Some people can get ready to play tennis or football in here.

H
> **Highgate Stadium**
> **Under-14s' hockey match**
> **2 p.m. today**

PART 2

QUESTIONS 6–10

Read the sentences about going to a concert.

Choose the best word (**A**, **B** or **C**) for each space.

For questions **6–10**, mark **A**, **B** or **C** on your answer sheet.

Example:

0   My friends and I .... to a rock concert last night.

    A   followed   **B**   went   **C**   arrived   *Answer:*

0	A	B	C
	☐	■	☐

---

6   The concert began at seven and we didn't want to be ....

    A   late   **B**   soon   **C**   already

7   At the concert, we .... the words to most of the songs.

    A   believed   **B**   knew   **C**   thought

8   The music was very .... so we couldn't chat to one another.

    A   full   **B**   hard   **C**   loud

9   The band .... on stage for over two hours.

    A   stayed   **B**   passed   **C**   spent

10   We all .... a great time at the concert.

    A   did   **B**   had   **C**   put

PART 3

QUESTIONS 11–15

Complete the five conversations.

For questions **11–15**, mark **A**, **B** or **C** on your answer sheet.

Example:

0

		Where do you come from?		**A** New York.
				B School.
				C Home.

Answer: 0 [A ■] [B □] [C □]

---

11 What about going to the cinema this evening?

    A I really enjoyed it.

    B I'm certain.

    C I'd love to.

12 We had a wonderful time on holiday.

    A Where did you go?

    B Why did you do that?

    C Have you been there?

13 If I buy a book for Mum, will you buy her some flowers?

    A But I've already got her something else.

    B If you do too.

    C Did you get them in town yesterday?

14 I'm sorry I forgot your birthday.

    A It's mine.

    B It doesn't matter.

    C It won't be.

15 What's your new teacher like?

    A Maths and tennis.

    B Three lessons a week.

    C Very nice, I think.

QUESTIONS 16–20

Complete the conversation.

What does Sara say to her mother?

For questions **16–20**, mark the correct letter **A–H** on your answer sheet.

Example:

Mother: Sara, please stop watching TV.

Sara: **0** ....D....   *Answer:* | **0** | A B C D E F G H
 ☐ ☐ ☐ ■ ☐ ☐ ☐ ☐ |

Mother:	Sorry, but I need you to come and help me now.		**A**	Shall I make a cake then?
Sara:	**16**		**B**	They've already done that.
Mother:	Help me with some cooking. I've got lots to do before Saturday.		**C**	Why? Is something special happening at the weekend?
Sara:	**17**			
Mother:	Your uncle and his family are going to visit us.		**D**	Just a bit longer, Mum.
Sara:	**18**		**E**	I made them a chocolate one.
Mother:	Well, they are and I need to get things ready.		**F**	Do you? What would you like me to do?
Sara:	**19**			
Mother:	Good idea. Have we got any eggs?		**G**	I think so. Yes, here they are.
Sara:	**20**		**H**	I didn't know they were coming.
Mother:	Great. You can get started then.			

PART 4

QUESTIONS 21–27

Read the article about a young swimmer.

Are sentences **21–27** 'Right' **(A)** or 'Wrong' **(B)**?

If there is not enough information to answer 'Right' **(A)** or 'Wrong' **(B)**, choose 'Doesn't say' **(C)**.

For questions **21–27**, mark **A**, **B** or **C** on your answer sheet.

Canada's top young swimmer

Greg Rye, the young Canadian swimmer, is becoming more and more famous. He has his own teacher, driver and even his own cook. Each time people hear him speak on television, they can't believe he's only 13. Greg's father is an engineer but he is also his son's manager. He says, 'I don't make Greg do anything he doesn't want to do. He chooses which competitions to swim in. But he works hard to keep fit and wins nearly every race he's in. I cut out all the newspaper articles about him and put them in a big box!'

Greg's phone rings several times a day because people want to write about him or photograph him for magazines. 'When I'm at school,' Greg says, 'I just want to be like my classmates. That's really important to me.' But Greg doesn't have a normal schoolboy's life. He often has to travel for international races and has little free time. 'I go to the pool every day and swim there for at least six hours. I get angry sometimes if I can't go to a party or spend time with friends because I have to swim or rest, but when I'm in the pool, I love every minute.'

Example:

0 A lot of people know who Greg Rye is.

    A Right   **B** Wrong   **C** Doesn't say   *Answer:*

0	A B C
	■ □ □

---

21 Greg has only been on TV once.

    A Right   **B** Wrong   **C** Doesn't say

22 People think that Greg is older than he really is.

    A Right   **B** Wrong   **C** Doesn't say

23 Greg's father works as an engineer three days a week.

    A Right   **B** Wrong   **C** Doesn't say

24 Greg's father tells him which races to swim in.

    A Right   **B** Wrong   **C** Doesn't say

25 Greg's father keeps the articles that journalists have written about his son.

    A Right   **B** Wrong   **C** Doesn't say

26 Greg is popular with his classmates.

    A Right   **B** Wrong   **C** Doesn't say

27 Greg always has time to go to parties with his friends.

    A Right   **B** Wrong   **C** Doesn't say

PART 5

QUESTIONS 28–35

Read the article about robots.

Choose the best word (**A**, **B** or **C**) for each space.

For questions **28–35**, mark **A**, **B** or **C** on your answer sheet.

Robots

Most people have seen films **(0)** .... robots, but robots are also used in real life. Robots can do **(28)** .... different things. They can, for example, make things in factories **(29)** .... help astronauts in space.

One new robot from Japan can **(30)** .... walk, run and climb stairs. Engineers hope that in the future **(31)** .... robot will be able to help people in their homes. **(32)** .... new robot is special because it can have a conversation **(33)** .... you.

A Canadian scientist has just **(34)** .... a robot that has hands that can move in 24 different ways. This is easy for people but **(35)** .... now it wasn't possible for a robot to do this.

Example:

0　**A** about　　　**B** in　　　**C** over　　　*Answer:*　| 0 | A ■ B □ C □ |

28　**A** lots　　　**B** much　　　**C** many

29　**A** or　　　**B** because　　　**C** if

30　**A** ever　　　**B** even　　　**C** yet

31　**A** some　　　**B** this　　　**C** these

32　**A** Other　　　**B** Both　　　**C** Another

33　**A** for　　　**B** to　　　**C** with

34　**A** made　　　**B** making　　　**C** makes

35　**A** since　　　**B** until　　　**C** from

PART 6

QUESTIONS 36–40

Read the descriptions of some words about health and the body.

What is the word for each one?

The first letter is already there. There is one space for each other letter in the word.

For questions **36–40**, write the words on your answer sheet.

Example:

0 This person can help you if you don't feel well.   d _ _ _ _ _

Answer:

0	doctor

---

36 You have to look in the mirror to see this part of your body. **f** _ _ _

37 If you have long hair, you need to use this every day. **b** _ _ _ _ _

38 If you eat this fruit once a day you will stay healthy. **a** _ _ _ _ _

39 People use this to wash themselves. **s** _ _ _

40 People are taken to hospital in this when they are ill. **a** _ _ _ _ _ _ _ _

PART 7

QUESTIONS 41–50

Complete the email.

Write ONE word for each space.

For questions **41–50**, write the words on your answer sheet.

Example: | **0** | *b e* |

| **From:** | Ivan |
| **To:** | Roberto |

Hi Roberto,

It'll **(0)** ………… my 12th birthday on June 18th. We are **(41)** ………… to have a barbecue at the lake. We'll have **(42)** ………… fun there than at the park. Would you **(43)** ………… to come? My dad will take us there **(44)** ………… car and he says I can invite some **(45)** ………… my friends.

Janet has already said she can come and I'm also inviting Ian **(46)** ………… you. You don't **(47)** ………… to bring anything to **(48)** ………… or drink because my mum will make a picnic.

(49) ………… it's warm and sunny we will go for a swim in the lake, so don't forget **(50)** ………… bring your swimming things.

PART 8

QUESTIONS 51–55

Read the website advertisement and the email.

Fill in the information in Mark's notes.

For questions **51–55**, write the information on your answer sheet.

Top Two Books
this month:

Forest Street
by Alan Banks
and
Best Bike Rides
by Kim James

**Order before 10th April for
special price for both books – £20**
www.booksalot.com

From:	Tony
To:	Mark

Let's get Laurie a book for his birthday. The new cycling book which is on sale at www.booksalot.com looks good, but it must arrive before April 12th, so can you order it online tonight?

It's £12.90 so that will cost us £6.45 each. Is that OK? I'll give you the money next week. Get them to post it to 39 West Road.

Thanks.

MARK'S NOTES

Laurie's birthday present

Website:	www.booksalot.com
Name of book:	**51**
Writer:	**52**
Date needed by:	**53**
Address to send book to:	**54**
Price of book:	**55** £

PART 9

QUESTION 56

You went to a friend's house yesterday and you left your bag there.
Write an email to your English friend, Jay.

Say:
- **what colour** the bag is
- **what** is **inside** the bag
- **where** in the house **you left it**.

Write **25–35** words.
Write the email on your answer sheet.

PAPER 2 LISTENING (approximately 30 minutes including 8 minutes transfer time)

PART 1

QUESTIONS 1–5

You will hear five short conversations.

You will hear each conversation twice.

There is one question for each conversation.

For each question, choose the right answer (**A**, **B** or **C**).

Example:

Which is the girl's horse?

(A)   B   C

---

1   What's Sally doing now?

A   B   C

2   Where did the woman find the ball?

A   B   C

3   How will Bella get to her friend's house this afternoon?

A   **B**   **C**

4   What job does Mark's sister do?

A   **B**   **C**

5   What's the date of Adrian's birthday party?

A   **B**   **C**

PART 2

QUESTIONS 6–10

Listen to Sam talking to a friend about his family.

Which sport does each person do now?

For questions **6–10**, write a letter **A–H** next to each person.

You will hear the conversation twice.

Example:

0   grandfather   F

PEOPLE

6   father

7   brother

8   uncle

9   sister

10   mother

SPORTS THEY DO NOW

A   climbing

B   football

C   hockey

D   sailing

E   skiing

F   swimming

G   tennis

H   volleyball

PART 3

QUESTIONS 11–15

Listen to Emma talking to a friend about her photography course.

For each question, choose the right answer (**A**, **B** or **C**).

You will hear the conversation twice.

Example:

0 Where does Emma do her photography course?

    A   Parkplace School

    (**B**) Riverside School

    C   West School

---

11   The photography classes start at

    A   2.00 p.m.

    B   2.30 p.m.

    C   2.45 p.m.

12   Emma's photography course costs

    A   £45.

    B   £65.

    C   £80.

13   Emma likes the course because she's

    A   learning about famous photographers.

    B   using an expensive camera.

    C   taking better photographs.

14 Emma thinks it's easy to take photographs of

    A flowers.

    B animals.

    C people.

15 What does Emma want to do after the course?

    A buy a digital camera

    B take photos for a competition

    C show her photos to her friends

PART 4

QUESTIONS 16–20

You will hear a boy, Richard, talking to a friend about visiting the circus.

Listen and complete each question.

You will hear the conversation twice.

Going to the Circus

Name of circus:	*Zippo's*
Day of circus visit:	**(16)** ....
Time show finishes:	**(17)** .... *p.m.*
Travel there by:	**(18)** ....
Cost of a ticket:	**(19)** £ ....
Take:	**(20)** ....

PART 5

QUESTIONS 21–25

You will hear a teacher giving some information about a trip to a museum.

Listen and complete each question.

You will hear the information twice.

Museum Trip

Name of museum: The Fashion Museum

Time bus leaves: **(21)** .... a.m.

At 2 p.m. see: **(22)** fashion ....

Must take: **(23)** ....

Cost of my ticket: **(24)** £ ....

Date of trip: **(25)** ....

You now have 8 minutes to write your answers on the answer sheet.

PAPER 3 SPEAKING (8–10 minutes)

The Speaking test lasts 8 to 10 minutes. You will take the test with another candidate. There are two examiners, but only one of them will talk to you. The examiner will ask you questions and ask you to talk to the other candidate.

Part 1 (5–6 minutes)

The examiner will ask you and your partner some questions. These questions will be about your daily life, past experience and future plans. For example, you may have to speak about your school, hobbies or home town.

Part 2 (3–4 minutes)

You and your partner will speak to each other. You will ask and answer questions. The examiner will give you a card with some information on it. The examiner will give your partner a card with some words on it. Your partner will use the words on the card to ask you questions about the information you have. Then you will change roles.

Test 2

PAPER 1   READING AND WRITING   (1 hour 10 minutes)

PART 1

QUESTIONS 1–5

Which notice (A–H) says this (1–5)?

For questions 1–5, mark the correct letter A–H on your answer sheet.

Example:

0   There is nobody at work here in the middle of the day.

Answer:

0	A	B	C	D	E	F	G	H
	☐	☐	☐	☐	☐	☐	■	☐

---

1   Young people and their parents may choose different meals.

A

> There is no restaurant on today's 12.30 train

B

> This way to the restaurant garden

2   People who are travelling can get something to eat here.

C

> Alco Department Store
> Half-price cups and glasses
> Today only

D

> Station Café
> Open all day
> Opposite ticket office

3   If you need some of these for your kitchen, you should buy them now.

E

> **CITY SCHOOL**
> Indian and Chinese
> cooking lessons begin Monday

4   You may get a present when you eat here.

F

> *Riverside Restaurant*
> Ask the waiter for our
> special children's menu

5   You can learn how to make different kinds of food here.

G

> School office closed for lunch
> between 1 p.m. and 2 p.m.

H

> **Marco's Pizzeria**
> Free toy with every
> under-12's meal

PART 2

QUESTIONS 6–10

Read the sentences about a girl who likes volleyball.

Choose the best word (**A**, **B** or **C**) for each space.

For questions **6–10**, mark **A**, **B** or **C** on your answer sheet.

Example:

0   Diana .... a lot of time playing volleyball for her school.

   A   spends   **B**   uses   **C**   gives   *Answer:* | 0 | A B C ■ ☐ ☐ |

---

6   Diana's team .... volleyball three times a week.

   A   exercises   **B**   practises   **C**   tries

7   At a match last week, Diana won a silver .... for being the best player.

   A   cup   **B**   glass   **C**   can

8   Diana sometimes has to .... school when her team travels to play against other teams.

   A   fail   **B**   lose   **C**   miss

9   Diana is .... that her team will do well this year.

   A   certain   **B**   careful   **C**   correct

10   Diana would like to .... a famous sportswoman one day.

   A   start   **B**   get   **C**   become

PART 3

QUESTIONS 11–15

Complete the five conversations.
For questions **11–15**, mark **A**, **B** or **C** on your answer sheet.

Example:

0

Where do you come from?

A New York.

B School.

C Home.

Answer: | **0** | A B C ■ ☐ ☐ |

---

11 Do you play a lot of tennis?

    A Only with my cousin.
    B It wasn't very long.
    C I've played it before!

12 Oh no, I've lost my mobile phone!

    A Have you seen it before?
    B Have you looked in your bag?
    C Have you got it?

13 Can you help me with the maths homework?

    A It's not ready.
    B Why can't you?
    C I don't understand it myself.

14 I'm hungry. Let's go for something to eat.

    A Quite sure!
    B Good idea!
    C It's great!

15 Can I go out this evening, Mum?

    A Can you tell me which one?
    B If you go there first.
    C Where do you want to go?

QUESTIONS 16–20

Complete the telephone conversation between two friends.

What does Mark say to Josh?

For questions **16–20**, mark the correct letter **A–H** on your answer sheet.

Example:

Josh: Hi Mark. What are you doing this evening?

Mark: **0** ....**E**.....   *Answer:* | **0** | A B C D E F G H ☐☐☐☐■☐☐☐ |

Josh: Do you want to go to the cinema later?

Mark: **16** ....

Josh: I'm not sure but we can go to the cinema and choose the best one.

Mark: **17** ....

Josh: OK. I'll see you as soon as I finish the maths homework.

Mark: **18** ....

Josh: OK, shall I come to your house at 7 p.m. then?

Mark: **19** ....

Josh: No problem, I'll do my homework quickly. How much money will I need?

Mark: **20** ....

Josh: Oh, great! See you later.

A   That won't take you long. I've already done it and it's easy.

B   It's OK, my mum's given me some money.

C   Do you like that cinema?

D   All right. Why don't you come to my house first and we'll walk there together.

E   Not much. Why?

F   Maybe. Do you know which films are showing?

G   It's a great film.

H   Can you get here a bit earlier than that?

PART 4

QUESTIONS 21–27

Read the article about some girls who play in a band.

Are sentences **21–27** 'Right' **(A)** or 'Wrong' **(B)**?

If there is not enough information to answer 'Right' **(A)** or 'Wrong' **(B)**, choose 'Doesn't say' **(C)**.

For questions **21–27**, mark **A**, **B** or **C** on your answer sheet.

Our Band

Fourteen-year-old Emma Peters talks about her new band

Soon it will be the summer holidays again. I'm not going away with my parents this year but I don't mind. I'm going to spend most of my time with two of my classmates, Bella and Lou.

We've just started a rock band which we call Sunshine. I play the guitar and sing, Bella plays the guitar and the keyboard and Lou plays the drums. We practise in Lou's dad's garage and we also play in music shops and local cafés. The band has been together for four months and we're all very good friends. I was in a different band last year but that wasn't so much fun. No one wanted to practise.

We've written several songs and we have our own website. Over the summer we are going to make a CD with ten or maybe twelve songs on it. We're not sure yet. We haven't finished writing all the songs, but we've decided on the name of the CD. We're going to call it *The Red Room*. The CD may not make us famous, but that doesn't matter – we just enjoy our music and sharing it with other people. I can't think of a better way to spend the summer.

Example:

0 Emma's summer holiday has already begun.

    A   Right   **B**   Wrong   **C**   Doesn't say   *Answer:*

0	A	B	C
	☐	■	☐

---

21 Emma would like to go somewhere with her family this summer.

    A   Right   **B**   Wrong   **C**   Doesn't say

22 Emma goes to the same school as the other members of the band, Sunshine.

    A   Right   **B**   Wrong   **C**   Doesn't say

23 Each of the three girls in the band plays an instrument.

    A   Right   **B**   Wrong   **C**   Doesn't say

24 The band is paid for playing in shops and cafés.

    A   Right   **B**   Wrong   **C**   Doesn't say

25 Emma says that her first band worked very hard.

    A   Right   **B**   Wrong   **C**   Doesn't say

26 The three girls have decided how many songs their CD will have.

    A   Right   **B**   Wrong   **C**   Doesn't say

27 The three girls hope their CD will make them famous.

    A   Right   **B**   Wrong   **C**   Doesn't say

PART 5

QUESTIONS 28–35

Read the article about learning to snowboard.

Choose the best word **(A, B** or **C)** for each space.

For questions **28–35**, mark **A, B** or **C** on your answer sheet.

Learning to snowboard

If you want to learn to snowboard, **(0)** .... first thing you need to do is book **(28)** .... lessons. It's a good idea to have lessons with a snowboard school **(29)** .... you need to learn the right way to snowboard. You will have much **(30)** .... fun learning with other people as well.

Indoor snow schools usually **(31)** .... you a snowboard, boots and a helmet to wear on your head **(32)** .... lessons. The indoor centres are cold and use real snow, so warm clothes are important. It's not a good idea to wear jeans because **(33)** .... get wet easily.

If you learn outside on a mountain, you **(34)** .... to take your own board and boots or rent them. You will **(35)** .... need sunglasses, gloves and a helmet.

Example:

0	**A** a	**B** one	**C** the	*Answer:*

		A B C
0		☐ ☐ ■

---

28   **A**   each   **B**   some   **C**   any

29   **A**   or   **B**   and   **C**   because

30   **A**   more   **B**   many   **C**   most

31   **A**   given   **B**   give   **C**   giving

32   **A**   during   **B**   among   **C**   into

33   **A**   them   **B**   their   **C**   they

34   **A**   must   **B**   have   **C**   can

35   **A**   too   **B**   quite   **C**   also

PART 6

QUESTIONS 36–40

Read the descriptions of some things you find in a living room.

What is the word for each one?

The first letter is already there. There is one space for each other letter in the word.

For questions **36–40**, write the words on your answer sheet.

Example:

0 You can watch programmes on this.   t _ _ _ _ _ _ _ _ _

	Answer:	**0**	t e l e v i s i o n

---

36 This is a comfortable seat for two or more people.   s _ _ _

37 If you want to know the time, you need to look at this.   c _ _ _ _

38 This usually has green leaves and you can grow it inside   p _ _ _ _
        a house.

39 People turn this on when it is dark.   l _ _ _ _

40 If you have a drink or snack, you can put it down on this. t _ _ _ _

PART 7

QUESTIONS 41–50

Complete the email.

Write ONE word for each space.

For questions **41–50**, write the words on your answer sheet.

Example: | **0** | *f o r* |

| **From:** | Lara |
| **To:** | Rebecca |

Hi Rebecca,

Thank you **(0)** .... your email. **(41)** .... you busy on Saturday? **(42)** .... you like to come shopping with me? My cousin is **(43)** .... to have a party at her place **(44)** .... week and I don't have anything nice to wear.

I want to buy a new pair **(45)** .... jeans and maybe a T-shirt as well. **(46)** .... you know a good shop? It has **(47)** .... be quite a cheap place because I've only got £25.

(48) .... you can come, I'll meet you at your house. Is the morning **(49)** .... afternoon better for you?

Text and let **(50)** .... know.

Lara

PART 8

QUESTIONS 51–55

Read the advertisement and the email.

Fill in the information in José's notes.

For questions **51–55**, write the information on your answer sheet.

**EXHIBITIONS
AT CITY MUSEUM**

10–14 June
Pyramid Treasures

18–21 June
Aztec Gold

Tickets:
Adult: £ 6.50
Students: £ 4.00

From:	Carlos
To:	José

The Pyramid Treasures exhibition has just finished so let's go to the Aztec Gold one – we can go on the exhibition's first day. It starts at 10 a.m. so I'll see you at the park nearby at 9.30 a.m. and we'll walk to the museum together. We can get the cheaper tickets because we're still at school.

JOSÉ'S NOTES

Exhibition visit

Place:	City Museum
Name of exhibition:	**51**
Date of visit:	**52**
My ticket price:	**53** £
Time to meet Carlos:	**54** a.m.
Place to meet Carlos:	**55**

PART 9

QUESTION 56

Yesterday you went to the sports stadium in your town.
Write an email to your English friend, Alex.

Say:
- **who went with you** to the stadium
- **which sport** you watched there
- **how long** you stayed there.

Write **25–35** words.
Write the email on your answer sheet.

PAPER 2 LISTENING (approximately 30 minutes including 8 minutes transfer time)

PART 1

QUESTIONS 1–5

You will hear five short conversations.

You will hear each conversation twice.

There is one question for each conversation.

For each question, choose the right answer (**A**, **B** or **C**).

Example:

Which is the girl's horse?

A

B

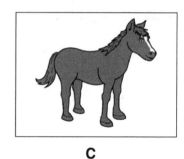

C

---

1 Where is William's mobile?

A

B

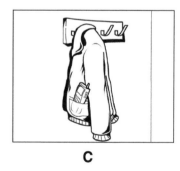

C

2 How much is a ticket for today's match?

£2.50	**£4.00**	**£5.00**
A	**B**	**C**

3   Which is the boy's sister?

   A   **B**   **C**

4   Where will they meet?

   A   **B**   **C**

5   What will they do this evening?

   A   **B**   **C**

PART 2

QUESTIONS 6–10

Listen to Sophie talking to her mother about presents for the family.

Which present will she buy for each person?

For questions **6–10**, write a letter **A–H** next to each person.

You will hear the conversation twice.

Example:

0   Nick   E

PEOPLE

6   Dad

7   Uncle Tim

8   Grandpa

9   Max

10   Ben

PRESENTS

A   hat

B   jacket

C   pen

D   shirt

E   socks

F   sweater

G   T-shirt

H   watch

PART 3

QUESTIONS 11–15

Listen to Jay talking to a friend about a holiday he went on with his family.

For each question, choose the right answer (**A**, **B** or **C**).

You will hear the conversation twice.

Example:

0 Jay came back from holiday on

   A Friday.

   B Saturday.

   (C) Sunday.

---

11 The hotel Jay stayed in was

   A in a city centre.

   B near the sea.

   C in the mountains.

12 Jay often spent his time

   A playing tennis.

   B swimming.

   C playing golf.

13 Jay's room had

   A a computer.

   B a fridge.

   C a television.

14   Jay ate a lot of

    A   pasta.

    B   fish.

    C   salads.

15   Jay's parents thought the hotel was

    A   too expensive.

    B   very comfortable.

    C   too noisy.

PART 4

QUESTIONS 16–20

You will hear Maria talking to her teacher about a school hockey competition.

Listen and complete each question.

You will hear the conversation twice.

Hockey Competition

Day of competition: Tuesday

Arrive at school at: **(16)** .... a.m.

High School teacher's name: **(17)** Mr ....

Take players to: **(18)** school ....

Bring: **(19)** £ .... for a snack

Number of schools in competition: **(20)** ....

PART 5

QUESTIONS 21–25

You will hear a man leaving a message about a bike.

Listen and complete each question.

You will hear the information twice.

Message

Name of person calling:	John
Day to collect bike:	(21) ....
Colour of bike:	(22) ....
Price of bike:	(23) £ ....
Address to go to:	(24) .... North Street
Time shop closes:	(25) .... p.m.

You now have 8 minutes to write your answers on the answer sheet.

PAPER 3   SPEAKING   (8–10 minutes)

The Speaking test lasts 8 to 10 minutes. You will take the test with another candidate. There are two examiners, but only one of them will talk to you. The examiner will ask you questions and ask you to talk to the other candidate.

Part 1 (5–6 minutes)

The examiner will ask you and your partner some questions. These questions will be about your daily life, past experience and future plans. For example, you may have to speak about your school, hobbies or home town.

Part 2 (3–4 minutes)

You and your partner will speak to each other. You will ask and answer questions. The examiner will give you a card with some information on it. The examiner will give your partner a card with some words on it. Your partner will use the words on the card to ask you questions about the information you have. Then you will change roles.

Test 3

PAPER 1   READING AND WRITING   (1 hour 10 minutes)

PART 1

QUESTIONS 1–5

Which notice **(A–H)** says this **(1–5)**?

For questions **1–5**, mark the correct letter **A–H** on your answer sheet.

Example:

0   You don't have to pay for your drink.   *Answer:*   **0**   A B C D E F G H

---

1   You can learn to cook here.

A   Volleyball team needs 3 more players
Call John Linton (660581)

2   It will not be possible to buy food
here this morning.

B   **Today only**
Free can of lemonade
with all burger meals

3   Talk to this person if you are interested
in this sport.

C   **DANGER**
No cooking on fires or
barbecues on this beach

D   SCHOOL SNACK SHOP ONLY OPEN
12 – 3 P.M. TODAY

4   You can buy healthy drinks in this place.

E   Green's Sports Club
New exercise class
Join now – all ages welcome

5   If you want to get fit, go here to become
a member.

F   **Hockey Team Meeting**
Saturday, 10 a.m.
All players must come!

G   **Fruit Juice Bar**
Special today –
banana and white grape

H   **Newtown School**
Course starts Saturday
Making Italian food

PART 2

QUESTIONS 6–10

Read the sentences about a boy who likes cars.

Choose the best word **(A, B** or **C)** for each space.

For questions **6–10**, mark **A, B** or **C** on your answer sheet.

Example:

0   Victor's .... lesson at school is science.

    A   favourite   **B**   popular   **C**   excellent   *Answer:*

0	A	B	C
	■	☐	☐

---

6   Last week, Victor's science teacher .... to the class how cars work.

    A   spoke   **B**   explained   **C**   said

7   Victor's class now know about different .... of car engines.

    A   ways   **B**   things   **C**   kinds

8   Victor has .... posters of cars all over his bedroom walls.

    A   put   **B**   made   **C**   taken

9   Victor .... last Saturday morning cleaning his dad's new sports car.

    A   kept   **B**   spent   **C**   left

10   When Victor is older he .... to be a racing driver or an engineer.

    A   believes   **B**   thinks   **C**   hopes

PART 3

QUESTIONS 11–15

Complete the five conversations.

For questions **11–15**, mark **A**, **B** or **C** on your answer sheet.

Example:

0

Where do you come from?

A New York.

B School.

C Home.

Answer: **0** A B C ■ ☐ ☐

---

11 Are you feeling better today?

    A Much, thanks.
    B Most of it.
    C More than me.

12 I've lost my school bag.

    A Are you sure?
    B I don't think it is.
    C How do you do?

13 What shall we do when we get to the park?

    A We have to walk to it.
    B We will do some of them.
    C We can play tennis.

14 I didn't see you on the bus this morning.

    A It was very quick.
    B I walked here today.
    C I didn't see it.

15 Why don't you send her an email?

    A I'd like to read it.
    B I'll do it now.
    C It's better than that one.

QUESTIONS 16–20

Complete the conversation between two friends.

What does Chris say to Nick?

For questions **16–20**, mark the correct letter **A–H** on your answer sheet.

Example:

Nick: Hello, Chris. How are you?

Chris: **0** ....F......

Answer:

	0	A B C D E F G H
		☐ ☐ ☐ ☐ ☐ ■ ☐ ☐

Nick: Not bad, but I've got a lot of maths homework to do tonight.

Chris: **16** ....

Nick: My laptop's broken. I'm going to Jack's house to use his.

Chris: **17** ....

Nick: It's quite a long bus journey from here.

Chris: **18** ....

Nick: Are you sure? Don't you need it this evening?

Chris: **19** ....

Nick: Really? That sounds great. And you're good at maths.

Chris: **20** ....

Nick: You'll be able to help me, of course!

A   I suppose I am, but why do you say that?

B   How far away is that?

C   It's easier than everything else.

D   What's wrong with your computer?

E   So why aren't you at home doing it now?

F   OK thanks, Nick. And you?

G   It's fine, I can use my brother's instead.

H   Well, my house is nearer. Why don't you come and use my computer?

PART 4

QUESTIONS 21–27

Read the article about a young girl who enjoys riding a BMX bike.

Are sentences **21–27** 'Right' **(A)** or 'Wrong' **(B)**?

If there is not enough information to answer 'Right' **(A)** or 'Wrong' **(B)**, choose 'Doesn't say' **(C)**.

For questions **21–27**, mark **A**, **B** or **C** on your answer sheet.

BMX Racing

Lisa Hawkins loves riding her BMX bike and her dream is to go to the Olympics.

Lisa first got interested in BMX racing when she went to watch her cousins in a competition at the age of ten. She hired a bike there for a pound and immediately fell in love with the sport. 'It was the best pound I ever spent,' she says. Lisa is only 16 but she has already had lots of success, and got first prize in a world BMX competition last year.

BMX racing is quite a dangerous sport and last year Lisa broke her shoulder and her foot. This did not stop her wanting to do more competitions. She exercises every day. She rides her bike for three hours or more and sometimes she goes to the gym or the swimming pool as well.

Like many sports people, Lisa believes in luck as well as hard work. 'My mother gave me a toy rabbit and I took it to the first competition that I won. Now I take it with me everywhere I go. I'm sure that it brings me luck because the one day I left it at home, I broke my foot!'

Example:

0   Lisa Hawkins raced at the last Olympics.

   A   Right   **B**   Wrong   **C**   Doesn't say   *Answer:*

---

21   Lisa is the only person in her family who rides a BMX.

   A   Right   **B**   Wrong   **C**   Doesn't say

22   Lisa liked the sport the first time she tried it.

   A   Right   **B**   Wrong   **C**   Doesn't say

23   Lisa has already won an international BMX competition.

   A   Right   **B**   Wrong   **C**   Doesn't say

24   Lisa was riding her favourite bike when she had an accident.

   A   Right   **B**   Wrong   **C**   Doesn't say

25   Lisa cycles less than three hours every day.

   A   Right   **B**   Wrong   **C**   Doesn't say

26   Lisa's mother always goes to competitions with her.

   A   Right   **B**   Wrong   **C**   Doesn't say

27   Lisa once forgot to take her lucky rabbit with her.

   A   Right   **B**   Wrong   **C**   Doesn't say

PART 5

QUESTIONS 28–35

Read the article about sleep.

Choose the best word (**A**, **B** or **C**) for each space.

For questions **28–35**, mark **A**, **B** or **C** on your answer sheet.

Teenagers and sleep

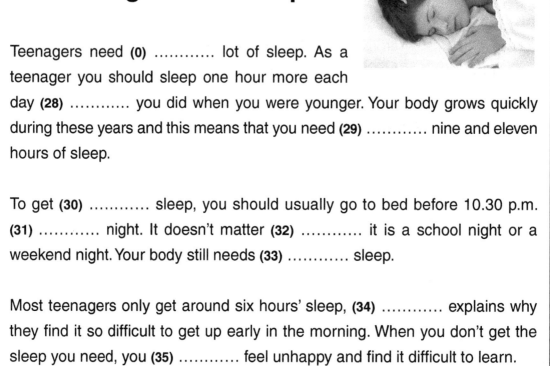

Teenagers need **(0)** .... lot of sleep. As a teenager you should sleep one hour more each day **(28)** .... you did when you were younger. Your body grows quickly during these years and this means that you need **(29)** .... nine and eleven hours of sleep.

To get **(30)** .... sleep, you should usually go to bed before 10.30 p.m. **(31)** .... night. It doesn't matter **(32)** .... it is a school night or a weekend night. Your body still needs **(33)** .... sleep.

Most teenagers only get around six hours' sleep, **(34)** .... explains why they find it so difficult to get up early in the morning. When you don't get the sleep you need, you **(35)** .... feel unhappy and find it difficult to learn.

Example:

0   **A**   the   **B**   a   **C**   one   *Answer:* | **0** | A B C ☐ ■ ☐ |

---

28   **A**   than   **B**   like   **C**   as

29   **A**   from   **B**   until   **C**   between

30   **A**   enough   **B**   many   **C**   another

31   **A**   some   **B**   every   **C**   all

32   **A**   so   **B**   because   **C**   if

33   **A**   its   **B**   his   **C**   their

34   **A**   that   **B**   which   **C**   who

35   **A**   must   **B**   should   **C**   may

PART 6

QUESTIONS 36–40

Read the descriptions of some places in a city.

What is the word for each one?

The first letter is already there. There is one space for each other letter in the word.

For questions **36–40**, write the words on your answer sheet.

Example:

0   Students are taught in classrooms here.   c _ _ _ _ _ _

	Answer:	**0**	*college*

---

36   If you have a special card, you can take books home
from here.   l _ _ _ _ _ _

37   You can order a meal in this place.   r _ _ _ _ _ _ _ _ _

38   This is a large building and things like cars are made here.   f _ _ _ _ _ _

39   You can look at interesting old things in this building.   m _ _ _ _ _

40   This store sells everything you need for cooking
and cleaning.   s _ _ _ _ _ _ _ _ _ _

PART 7

QUESTIONS 41–50

Complete the message left on the internet.

Write ONE word for each space.

For questions **41–50**, write the words on your answer sheet.

Example: | **0** | is |

My name **(0)** ………… Teresa Lopez. I live in the centre of Buenos Aires and I'm twelve **(41)** ………… a half years old.

I enjoy school. I'm good **(42)** ………… music and languages but I hate history. The lessons **(43)** ………… so boring. When I'm older, I want to **(44)** ………… a film star or a dancer but my parents **(45)** ………… not think that's a good idea!

I like meeting lots **(46)** ………… different people, and I'd like to travel all around the world. I **(47)** ………… only been to the USA, but next summer I hope **(48)** ………… visit Europe. That's why I'm looking **(49)** ………… a penfriend in England.

Please send me an email and tell me **(50)** ………… your family and your hobbies.

PART 8

QUESTIONS 51–55

Read the notice and the email.

Fill in the information on the class trip booking form.

For questions **51–55**, write the information on your answer sheet.

CLASS TRIP

February 28 – Fashion Show
OR
March 3 – Leeds Castle

Each trip costs £14
No more than £5 spending money please

Bus leaves from school at 7.30 a.m.

Phone School Secretary (441553)
for more information.

From:	Becky Elliott
To:	Emma Watson

I can't come to school tomorrow. Can you fill in my class trip form? I think the fashion show sounds better than the castle trip and please give them mum's work number (287229). I usually prefer travelling by train but this bus journey will be OK because it won't take long.

CLASS TRIP BOOKING FORM

Student's name: Becky Elliott

Trip to: **51**

Travel by: **52**

Date: **53**

Price: **54** £

Parent's phone number: **55**

PART 9

QUESTION 56

Read the email from your English friend, Alex.

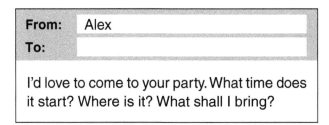

From:	Alex
To:	

I'd love to come to your party. What time does it start? Where is it? What shall I bring?

Write an email to Alex and answer the questions.

Write **25–35** words.

Write the email on your answer sheet.

PAPER 2 LISTENING (approximately 30 minutes including 8 minutes transfer time)

PART 1

QUESTIONS 1–5

You will hear five short conversations.

You will hear each conversation twice.

There is one question for each conversation.

For each question, choose the right answer (**A**, **B** or **C**).

Example:

Which is the girl's horse?

  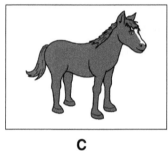

A   **B**   **C**

---

1   What doesn't the girl like about her photo?

A   **B**   **C**

2   What will Tim do first?

A   **B**   **C**

3   Which is the girl's next lesson?

         A   **B**   **C**

4   What is Sonia going to eat?

         A   **B**   **C**

5   What did Jack's mum give him for his birthday?

         A   **B**   **C**

PART 2

QUESTIONS 6–10

Listen to Lucy talking to a friend about a new sports centre.

What is the problem with the different places at the sports centre?

For questions **6–10**, write a letter **A–H** next to each place.

You will hear the conversation twice.

Example:

0 swimming pool `C`

PLACES		PROBLEMS	
6 car park		**A**	big
7 café		**B**	boring
8 sports shop		**C**	crowded
9 dance club		**D**	dirty
10 basketball club		**E**	early
		F	expensive
		G	hot
		H	small

PART 3

QUESTIONS 11–15

Listen to Simon talking to a friend about a school trip.

For each question, choose the right answer (**A**, **B** or **C**).

You will hear the conversation twice.

Example:

0   Simon went on a school trip on

    A   Monday.

    B   Tuesday.

    (C)   Wednesday.

---

11   In the morning, Simon visited the

    A   science museum.

    B   motorbike factory.

    C   TV centre.

12   Simon thought the TV centre was too

    A   hot.

    B   crowded.

    C   noisy.

13   Simon bought

    A   a T-shirt.

    B   a sandwich.

    C   a poster.

14   Simon enjoyed listening to a talk about

    A   music.

    B   space travel.

    C   clocks.

15   Simon took photographs of

    A   a park.

    B   his friends.

    C   a motorbike.

PART 4

QUESTIONS 16–20

You will hear a girl speaking on the telephone.

Listen and complete each question.

You will hear the conversation twice.

Message

To:	Amy
From:	(16) ....
About:	Shopping trip
Leave at:	(17) .... a.m.
Travel by:	(18) ....
Take:	(19) .... things
	(20) and ....

PART 5

QUESTIONS 21–25

You will hear a man talking on the radio about a competition to win concert tickets.
Listen and complete each question.
You will hear the information twice.

Radio Competition to win Concert Tickets

Win tickets to see:	Metro
Date of concert:	(21) ....
Place:	(22) ....
Type of music:	(23) ....
Phoning the radio programme	
Phone number:	(24) ....
Last day to phone:	(25) ....

You now have 8 minutes to write your answers on the answer sheet.

PAPER 3   SPEAKING   (8–10 minutes)

The Speaking test lasts 8 to 10 minutes. You will take the test with another candidate. There are two examiners, but only one of them will talk to you. The examiner will ask you questions and ask you to talk to the other candidate.

Part 1 (5–6 minutes)

The examiner will ask you and your partner some questions. These questions will be about your daily life, past experience and future plans. For example, you may have to speak about your school, hobbies or home town.

Part 2 (3–4 minutes)

You and your partner will speak to each other. You will ask and answer questions. The examiner will give you a card with some information on it. The examiner will give your partner a card with some words on it. Your partner will use the words on the card to ask you questions about the information you have. Then you will change roles.

Test 4

PAPER 1   READING AND WRITING   (1 hour 10 minutes)

PART 1

QUESTIONS 1–5

Which notice **(A–H)** says this **(1–5)**?

For questions **1–5**, mark the correct letter **A–H** on your answer sheet.

Example:

0   You cannot talk in here.

Answer:

	A B C D E F G H
0	☐ ☐ ☐ ☐ ☐ ☐ ■ ☐

---

1   This may be the cheapest place to buy these.

A
> Dictionary found
> See school secretary

B
> Ask at reception
> before putting anything on
> the noticeboard

2   You should put everything back in the right place.

C
> **Study Centre**
> Return books / CDs
> to correct shelf after use

3   You cannot buy anything here today.

D
> City Library – TODAY
> Richard Holt will read
> from his latest book

4   If you have lost a book, go and see this person.

E
> **All Students**
> Return textbooks to teachers
> at end of term

F
> **Today only**
> All children's books half-price

5   You can listen to a writer here.

G
> ALL STUDENTS
> Please be quiet in the library

H
> COLLEGE BOOKSHOP
> CLOSED UNTIL MONDAY

PART 2

QUESTIONS 6–10

Read the sentences about Emily's birthday.

Choose the best word (**A**, **B** or **C**) for each space.

For questions **6–10**, mark **A**, **B** or **C** on your answer sheet.

Example:

0   Yesterday, Emily was very .... because it was her
fourteenth birthday.

   A   happy   **B**   afraid   **C**   surprised   *Answer:*   [0 | A ■ B ☐ C ☐]

---

6   Emily's parents gave her a new bicycle which she can .... to school every day.

   A   go   **B**   drive   **C**   ride

7   Emily .... three of her friends to meet her in town.

   A   agreed   **B**   invited   **C**   explained

8   Emily and her friends had a .... in a café and then they went shopping.

   A   meal   **B**   food   **C**   dish

9   Emily and her friends then .... the evening watching a DVD at her house.

   A   gave   **B**   spent   **C**   took

10   Emily said it was the most .... birthday ever.

   A   favourite   **B**   popular   **C**   exciting

PART 3

QUESTIONS 11–15

Complete the five conversations.

For questions **11–15**, mark **A**, **B** or **C** on your answer sheet.

Example:

0

Where do you come from?

A New York.

B School.

C Home.

Answer:

| 0 | A ■ | B ☐ | C ☐ |

---

11 Shall I make some hot chocolate?

    A Yes, of course it is.

    B I do too.

    C That's a good idea.

12 I thought the film was really boring.

    A If you like.

    B So did I.

    C I'm afraid not.

13 Are you free this Tuesday?

    A Not very often.

    B Not until the evening.

    C Not long now.

14 I'll wait for you outside the stadium.

    A Can we meet somewhere else?

    B Do you know how to do it?

    C Are you sure you went there?

15 Have you got this T-shirt in a larger size?

    A I haven't seen it.

    B I think you will be.

    C I'll go and check for you.

QUESTIONS 16–20

Complete the conversation between two friends.

What does Luke say to David?

For questions **16–20**, mark the correct letter **A–H** on your answer sheet.

Example:

David:	Hi, Luke. Do you want to come and watch the hockey game this evening?
Luke:	**0** .....C.....

Answer:

David:	Good. Let's meet in the entrance to the sports hall.
Luke:	**16** ....
David:	It doesn't begin until seven, but can you get there by six?
Luke:	**17** ....
David:	We'll get good seats at the front if we do that.
Luke:	**18** ....
David:	I don't know yet, but they won't be expensive.
Luke:	**19** ....
David:	Yes! I spoke to them this afternoon. Do you know anyone else who would like to come?
Luke:	**20** ....
David:	OK. I'll call him now.

A   Great idea! How much are the tickets?

B   No, that bus goes at twenty past.

C   Yes, that sounds great!

D   That's good. Are Pat and Thomas going too?

E   I think John really enjoys watching hockey.

F   Me too! I'll have time to buy a burger in town.

G   OK. When does the game start?

H   That's not a problem. But why so early?

PART 4

QUESTIONS 21–27

Read the article about a career in film and then answer the questions.

Are sentences **21–27** 'Right' **(A)** or 'Wrong' **(B)**?

If there is not enough information to answer 'Right' **(A)** or 'Wrong' **(B)**, choose 'Doesn't say' **(C)**.

For questions **21–27**, mark **A**, **B** or **C** on your answer sheet.

Would you like a career in film?

Lana Carter has not worked in film for many years but she has already helped make several movies and worked with a few famous film stars.

Lana's job is to work the lights and the camera during filming. Sometimes, she also helps decide where movies are made. She has worked on all kinds of full-length movies and a variety of advertisements and music videos. She thinks making music videos is the easiest because they don't have to look or feel real. She says that working on movies is more difficult because lighting mistakes can make the whole thing look wrong.

Lana decided she would like to work in film when she was 16. Her friends and family laughed at the idea, but she found out about courses and did a university course in Film and Video. She says, 'You shouldn't worry about making mistakes at university. Try new ideas and don't just do the same as everyone else.' She thinks that people who want a career like hers should choose a course that lets them do as much filming as possible. 'Courses that just ask students to do a lot of writing are not useful to anybody.'

Example:

0   Lana Carter has had a long career in film.

    A   Right   **B**   Wrong   **C**   Doesn't say   *Answer:*   0   A B C

---

21   Lana has met some famous actors.

    A   Right   **B**   Wrong   **C**   Doesn't say

22   Lana likes planning where to make films most of all.

    A   Right   **B**   Wrong   **C**   Doesn't say

23   Lana believes that music videos are harder to make than movies.

    A   Right   **B**   Wrong   **C**   Doesn't say

24   Lana's family wanted her to have a career in film.

    A   Right   **B**   Wrong   **C**   Doesn't say

25   Lana was one of the best students on her course at university.

    A   Right   **B**   Wrong   **C**   Doesn't say

26   Lana thinks it is fine for film students to make mistakes.

    A   Right   **B**   Wrong   **C**   Doesn't say

27   Lana thinks that writing is more important on courses than making films.

    A   Right   **B**   Wrong   **C**   Doesn't say

PART 5

QUESTIONS 28–35

Read the article about basketball.

Choose the best word (**A**, **B** or **C**) for each space.

For questions **28–35**, mark **A**, **B** or **C** on your answer sheet.

Basketball

Today, Americans watch more basketball **(0)** .... television than any other sport. But it is popular in **(28)** .... countries too. People often **(29)** .... it 'the international game' because it is played in almost **(30)** .... country of the world. But basketball is not an old sport like football, which people have played for centuries. People have only played basketball **(31)** .... 1891.

The idea for basketball came from James Naismith, a Canadian teacher, who wanted his students to learn **(32)** .... new kind of sport. Instead **(33)** .... the players kicking the ball **(34)** .... they do in soccer, in Naismith's new game, the players threw or bounced the ball. Then, they had to get **(35)** .... into a big bag or 'basket'. The name that Naismith chose for this new sport was 'basketball'.

Example:

| 0 | **A** on | **B** in | **C** to | *Answer:* | 0 | A ■ B ☐ C ☐ |

---

28 **A** another   **B** both   **C** other

29 **A** called   **B** call   **C** calling

30 **A** every   **B** both   **C** some

31 **A** before   **B** since   **C** until

32 **A** a   **B** the   **C** one

33 **A** at   **B** from   **C** of

34 **A** if   **B** as   **C** for

35 **A** it   **B** him   **C** them

PART 6

QUESTIONS 36–40

Read the descriptions of some things you may see in the countryside.

What is the word for each one?

The first letter is already there. There is one space for each other letter in the word.

For questions **36–40**, write the words on your answer sheet.

Example:

0   These fall from trees in the autumn when the weather gets colder.

l _ _ _ _ _

Answer: | **0** | l e a v e s

---

36   This grows on the ground and horses and sheep eat it.

g _ _ _ _

37   You usually see lots of tall trees in this place.

f _ _ _ _ _ _

38   You need to stand on a hill on a windy day to fly this.

k _ _ _

39   People come here to go fishing.

r _ _ _ _

40   This is very high and it can take a long time to walk to the top.

m _ _ _ _ _ _ _

PART 7

QUESTIONS 41–50

Complete the email.

Write ONE word for each space.

For questions **41–50**, write the words on your answer sheet.

Example: | **0** | i n |

| **From:** | Patrick |
| **To:** | Karl |

Hi!

At the moment I'm on holiday **(0)** .... Jamaica with my parents. We flew to this wonderful island two weeks **(41)** .... It is sunny every day. **(42)** .... week we saw most of the island because my dad rented a car.

We **(43)** .... staying at a lovely hotel **(44)** .... a swimming pool, but we often swim in the sea instead. I love swimming there because **(45)** .... water is so clear. I swam quite a long way yesterday and saw a **(46)** .... of beautiful fish. **(47)** .... were some amazing red and yellow fish and I took pictures of them.

Jamaica is **(48)** .... beautiful than anywhere else I've been to, and I don't want **(49)** .... come home! But school starts again at the end **(50)** .... August. So I'll see you then!

Patrick

PART 8

QUESTIONS 51–55

Read the advertisement and the email.

Fill in the information in Jo's notes.

For questions **51–55**, write the information on your answer sheet.

Star Phones
11 Market Street

SALE

Starts: 29 July
Finishes: 5 August

Mobile phones £55
– were £120

From:	Mike
To:	Jo

I know you want a new mobile so why don't we go to Star Phones, the store on Market Street, not the one on Bridge Street, on the first day of their sale? Their phones will be £65 cheaper then. There's a bus to the city centre at 8.10 so wait for me at the library at 7.45 and we'll walk to the bus station together.

Jo's Notes

Shopping Trip

Name of shop: Star Phones

Date of trip: **51**

Address of shop: **52**

Sale price of phones: **53** £

Place to meet Mike: **54**

Time bus leaves: **55** a.m.

PART 9

QUESTION 56

Read the email from your English friend, Robin.

From:	Robin
To:	

I really like listening to music. What kind of music do you like? Who is your favourite band? How many of their CDs do you have?

Write an email to Robin and answer the questions.
Write **25–35** words.
Write the email on your answer sheet.

PAPER 2 LISTENING (approximately 30 minutes including 8 minutes transfer time)

PART 1

QUESTIONS 1–5

You will hear five short conversations.

You will hear each conversation twice.

There is one question for each conversation.

For each question, choose the right answer **(A**, **B** or **C)**.

Example:

Which is the girl's horse?

A

B

C

---

1   What is Becky going to take for the picnic?

A

B

C

2   How much is the mobile phone?

A

B

C

3   Where will they buy the eggs?

A
B
C

4   What time does the film start?

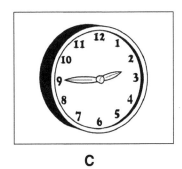

A
B
C

5   How will the boy travel to the beach?

A
B
C

PART 2

QUESTIONS 6–10

Listen to Rick and Helen talking about their friends and their favourite lessons.

What is each person's favourite lesson?

For questions **6–10**, write a letter **A–H** next to each person.

You will hear the conversation twice.

Example:

0   Helen | G |

PEOPLE

6   Rick   ☐

7   Paul   ☐

8   Sunita   ☐

9   Robert   ☐

10 Holly   ☐

FAVOURITE LESSONS

A   art

B   English

C   geography

D   history

E   maths

F   music

G   science

H   Spanish

PART 3

QUESTIONS 11–15

Listen to Joe talking to his mother about his day at school.

For each question, choose the right answer (**A**, **B** or **C**).

You will hear the conversation twice.

Example:

0   What time did Joe get home?

    A   3.45 p.m.

    (**B**)   4.00 p.m.

    C   4.15 p.m.

---

11   Where did Joe play football?

    A   in the park

    B   in the sports hall

    C   on the school field

12   Joe would like his mother to wash his

    A   socks and shorts.

    B   T-shirt and shorts.

    C   socks and T-shirt.

13   When is Joe's next football match?

    A   12 March

    B   15 March

    C   18 March

14   The team photo will cost Joe

  A   £2.25.

  B   £4.50.

  C   £6.75.

15   What homework must Joe do for tomorrow?

  A   science

  B   history

  C   maths

PART 4

QUESTIONS 16–20

You will hear a girl, Lucy, talking to a friend about visiting the cinema.

Listen and complete each question.

You will hear the conversation twice.

Cinema Visit

Name of cinema: Star Cinema

Day of cinema visit: **(16)** ....

Name of film: **(17)** ....

Place to meet: **(18)** ....

Time film begins: **(19)** .... *p.m.*

Cost of my ticket: **(20)** £ ....

PART 5

QUESTIONS 21–25

You will hear a teacher talking about a trip to the zoo.

Listen and complete each question.

You will hear the information twice.

Zoo Trip

Name of zoo: Westpark Zoo

Day of trip: **(21)** ....

Cost of trip: **(22)** £ ....

Meeting place for tour: **(23)** ....

At 3 p.m. see: **(24)** .... eat their food

Zoo shop sells: **(25)** .... and postcards

You now have 8 minutes to write your answers on the answer sheet.

PAPER 3 SPEAKING (8–10 minutes)

The Speaking test lasts 8 to 10 minutes. You will take the test with another candidate. There are two examiners, but only one of them will talk to you. The examiner will ask you questions and ask you to talk to the other candidate.

Part 1 (5–6 minutes)

The examiner will ask you and your partner some questions. These questions will be about your daily life, past experience and future plans. For example, you may have to speak about your school, hobbies or home town.

Part 2 (3–4 minutes)

You and your partner will speak to each other. You will ask and answer questions. The examiner will give you a card with some information on it. The examiner will give your partner a card with some words on it. Your partner will use the words on the card to ask you questions about the information you have. Then you will change roles.

Visual materials for Paper 3

1A

Future World
the amazing new computer game
Build a city in space

On Sale
from next week
in
computer shops and supermarkets

For 2–4 players
only £35!

2B

Ride at Adventure Park

- name / ride ?

- when / open ?

- what / see ?

- children's ticket ? £ ?

- where / buy tickets ?

3A

Free Lesson

Do you know how to repair your bike?

Sarah can teach you!

Come to 'The Bike Shop'

140 West Street

10 a.m. Saturday

Bring your bike!

4B

<u>Singing competition</u>

- when ?

- where ?

- age / singers ?

- what / win ?

- more information ? ☎ ?

1B

Computer game

- what / called ?

- expensive ?

- how many players ?

- where / buy ?

- buy / now ?

2A

New ride opens 5 May
at Adventure Park
See all the city from
The Big Wheel

Tickets on sale at park entrance
Adults: £3.50
Under 16s: £2.50

3B

Free lesson

- what / learn ?

- name / teacher ?

- where / lessons ?

- time ?

- take anything ?

4A

COMPETITION
Young Singer of the Year

York Concert Hall

May 29

Win a guitar!

Singers must be under 16

Want to know more? Call or text 998456

1C

TeenVoice

the new magazine for teenagers
£2

interesting stories and pages of fashion and music
on sale every week

go to
www.teenvoice.com
NOW

2D

Jeep ride

- where ?

- for children ?

- every day ?

- price ? £ ?

- what / wear ?

3C

Black's English School

29 Park Street

Learn to speak English in 2 hours a week

Beginners: 6 p.m. – 8 p.m. Wednesdays
Conversation classes: 9 a.m. – 11 a.m. Saturdays

£60 for 6 lessons

Call: 321703

4D

Television music channel

- name / channel ?

- what kind / music ?

- date / start ?

- what / see ?

- website ?

1D

Teenage magazine

- name / magazine ?

- website ?

- what / read about ?

- cost ? £ ?

- when / buy ?

2C

Jeep Rides
in the desert

Tuesdays and Saturdays
2 p.m. till 6 p.m.

£17.50 per person

Children must be over 12 years old

Bring hat and boots

3D

English lessons

* where ?

* conversation classes ?

* cost ?

* how long / lesson ?

* more information ? ☎ ?

4C

A great new TV channel:

MUSIC CHANNEL PLUS

starts 1 May

watch the latest music videos
and
listen to rock and hip-hop

*visit **www.music.com** for more information*

Paper 3 frames

Test 1

Note: The visual material for Paper 3 appears on pages 94–101.

Part 1 (5–6 minutes)

Greetings and introductions
At the beginning of Part 1, the interlocutor greets the candidates, asks for their names and asks them to spell something.

Giving information about place of origin, occupation, studies
The interlocutor asks the candidates about where they come from/live, and for information about their school/studies.

Giving general information about self
The interlocutor asks the candidates questions about their daily life, past experience or future plans. They may be asked, for example, about their likes and dislikes or about recent past experiences, or to describe and compare places.

Extended responses
In the final section of Part 1, candidates are expected to give an extended response to a 'Tell me something about …' prompt. The topics are still of a personal and concrete nature. Candidates should produce at least three utterances in their extended response.

Part 2 (3–4 minutes)

The interlocutor introduces the activity as follows:

Interlocutor: (Pablo), here is some information about a **computer game**.
(Interlocutor shows answer card 1A on page 94 to Pablo)

(Laura), you don't know anything about the **computer game**, so ask *(Pablo)* some questions about it.

(Interlocutor shows question card 1B on page 96 to Laura)

Use these words to help you. *(Interlocutor indicates prompt words)*

Do you understand?

Now *(Laura)*, ask *(Pablo)* your questions about the **computer game**, and *(Pablo)* you answer them.

1A

Future World
the amazing new computer game
Build a city in space

On Sale
from next week
in
computer shops and supermarkets

For 2–4 players
only £35!

1B

Computer game

- what / called ?

- expensive ?

- how many players ?

- when / buy ?

- buy / now ?

When the candidates have asked and answered their questions about the computer game, they then exchange roles and talk about a different topic.

The interlocutor introduces the activity as follows:

Interlocutor: *(Laura)*, here is some information about a **teenage magazine**.
(Interlocutor shows answer card 1C on page 98 to Laura)

(Pablo), you don't know anything about the **teenage magazine**, so ask *(Laura)* some questions about it.

(Interlocutor shows question card 1D on page 100 to Pablo)

Use these words to help you. *(Interlocutor indicates prompt words)*

Do you understand?

Now *(Pablo)*, ask *(Laura)* your questions about the **teenage magazine**, and *(Laura)* you answer them.

1C

TeenVoice

the new magazine for teenagers
£2

*interesting stories and pages of
fashion and music*
on sale every week

go to
www.teenvoice.com
NOW

1D

Teenage magazine

- name / magazine ?

- website ?

- what / read about ?

- cost / £ ?

- when / buy ?

Note: Candidates are assessed on both their questions and answers in Part 2 of the test.

Test 2

Note: The visual material for Paper 3 appears on pages 94–101.

Part 1 (5–6 minutes)

Greetings and introductions
At the beginning of Part 1, the interlocutor greets the candidates, asks for their names and asks them to spell something.

Giving information about place of origin, occupation, studies
The interlocutor asks the candidates about where they come from/live, and for information about their school/studies.

Giving general information about self
The interlocutor asks the candidates questions about their daily life, past experience or future plans. They may be asked, for example, about their likes and dislikes or about recent past experiences, or to describe and compare places.

Extended responses
In the final section of Part 1, candidates are expected to give an extended response to a 'Tell me something about …' prompt. The topics are still of a personal and concrete nature. Candidates should produce at least three utterances in their extended response.

Part 2 (3–4 minutes)

The interlocutor introduces the activity as follows:

Interlocutor: (Pablo), here is some information about a **ride at an adventure park**.
(Interlocutor shows answer card 2A on page 96 to Pablo)

(Laura), you don't know anything about the **ride at an adventure park**, so ask
(Pablo) some questions about it.

(Interlocutor shows question card 2B on page 94 to Laura)

Use these words to help you. *(Interlocutor indicates prompt words)*

Do you understand?

Now (Laura), ask (Pablo) your questions about the **ride at an adventure park**,
and (Pablo) you answer them.

<table>
<tr><td>

2A

New ride opens 5 May
at Adventure Park
See all the city from
The Big Wheel

Tickets on sale at park entrance
Adults: £3.50
Under 16s: £2.50

</td><td>

2B

Ride at Adventure Park

- name / ride ?

- when / open ?

- what / see ?

- children's ticket / £ ?

- where / buy tickets ?

</td></tr>
</table>

When the candidates have asked and answered their questions about a ride at an adventure
park, they then exchange roles and talk about a different topic.

The interlocutor introduces the activity as follows:

Interlocutor: *(Laura)*, here is some information about a **jeep ride**.
(Interlocutor shows answer card 2C on page 100 to Laura)

(Pablo), you don't know anything about the **jeep ride**, so ask
(Laura) some questions about it.

(Interlocutor shows question card 2D on page 98 to Pablo)

Use these words to help you. *(Interlocutor indicates prompt words)*

Do you understand?

Now *(Pablo)*, ask *(Laura)* your questions about the **jeep ride**, and
(Laura) you answer them.

2C

<u>Jeep Rides</u>
in the desert

Tuesdays and Saturdays
2 p.m. till 6 p.m.

£17.50 per person

Children must be over 12 years old

Bring hat and boots

2D

<u>Jeep ride</u>

- where ?

- for children ?

- every day ?

- price / £ ?

- what / wear ?

Note: Candidates are assessed on both their questions and answers in Part 2 of the test.

Test 3

Note: The visual material for Paper 3 appears on pages 94–101.

Part 1 (5–6 minutes)

Greetings and introductions
At the beginning of Part 1, the interlocutor greets the candidates, asks for their names and asks them to spell something.

Giving information about place of origin, occupation, studies
The interlocutor asks the candidates about where they come from/live, and for information about their school/studies.

Giving general information about self
The interlocutor asks the candidates questions about their daily life, past experience or future plans. They may be asked, for example, about their likes and dislikes or about recent past experiences, or to describe and compare places.

Extended responses
In the final section of Part 1, candidates are expected to give an extended response to a 'Tell me something about …' prompt. The topics are still of a personal and concrete nature. Candidates should produce at least three utterances in their extended response.

Part 2 (3–4 minutes)

The interlocutor introduces the activity as follows:

Interlocutor: (Pablo), here is some information about a **free lesson**.
(Interlocutor shows answer card 3A on page 95 to Pablo)

(Laura), you don't know anything about the **free lesson**, so ask
(Pablo) some questions about it.

(Interlocutor shows question card 3B on page 97 to Laura)

Use these words to help you. *(Interlocutor indicates prompt words)*

Do you understand?

Now *(Laura)*, ask *(Pablo)* your questions about the **free lesson**, and
(Pablo) you answer them.

3A

Free Lesson

Do you know how to repair your bike?

Sarah can teach you!

Come to 'The Bike Shop'

140 West Street

10 a.m. Saturday

Bring your bike!

3B

Free lesson

- what / learn ?

- name / teacher ?

- where / lessons ?

- time ?

- take anything ?

When the candidates have asked and answered their questions about the free lesson, they then
exchange roles and talk about a different topic.

The interlocutor introduces the activity as follows:

Interlocutor: *(Laura)*, here is some information about **English lessons**.
(Interlocutor shows answer card 3C on page 99 to Laura)

(Pablo), you don't know anything about the **English lessons**, so ask *(Laura)* some questions about them.

(Interlocutor shows question card 3D on page 101 to Pablo)

Use these words to help you. *(Interlocutor indicates prompt words)*

Do you understand?

Now *(Pablo)*, ask *(Laura)* your questions about the **English lessons**, and *(Laura)* you answer them.

3C

Black's English School

29 Park Street

Learn to speak English
in 2 hours a week

Beginners: 6 p.m. – 8 p.m.
Wednesdays
Conversation classes: 9 a.m. – 11 a.m.
Saturdays

£60 for 6 lessons

Call: 321703

3D

English lessons

- where ?

- conversation classes ?

- cost ?

- how long / lesson ?

- more information ? ☎ ?

Note: Candidates are assessed on both their questions and answers in Part 2 of the test.

Test 4

Note: The visual material for Paper 3 appears on pages 94–101.

Part 1 (5–6 minutes)

Greetings and introductions
At the beginning of Part 1, the interlocutor greets the candidates, asks for their names and asks them to spell something.

Giving information about place of origin, occupation, studies
The interlocutor asks the candidates about where they come from/live, and for information about their school/studies.

Giving general information about self
The interlocutor asks the candidates questions about their daily life, past experience or future plans. They may be asked, for example, about their likes and dislikes or about recent past experiences, or to describe and compare places.

Extended responses
In the final section of Part 1, candidates are expected to give an extended response to a 'Tell me something about …' prompt. The topics are still of a personal and concrete nature. Candidates should produce at least three utterances in their extended response.

Part 2 (3–4 minutes)

The interlocutor introduces the activity as follows:

Interlocutor: (*Pablo*), here is some information about a **singing competition**.
(*Interlocutor shows answer card 4A on page 97 to Pablo*)

(*Laura*), you don't know anything about the **singing competition**, so ask
(*Pablo*) some questions about it.

(*Interlocutor shows question card 4B on page 95 to Laura*)

Use these words to help you. (*Interlocutor indicates prompt words*)

Do you understand?

Now (*Laura*), ask (*Pablo*) your questions about the **singing competition**, and
(*Pablo*) you answer them.

4A

COMPETITION
Young Singer of the Year

York Concert Hall

May 29

Win a guitar!

Singers must be under 16

Want to know more?

Call or text 998456

4B

Singing competition

- when ?

- where ?

- age / singers ?

- what / win ?

- more information ? ☎ ?

When the candidates have asked and answered their questions about the singing competition,
they then exchange roles and talk about a different topic.

The interlocutor introduces the activity as follows:

Interlocutor: (*Laura*), here is some information about a **television music channel**.
(Interlocutor shows answer card 4C on page 101 to Laura)

(*Pablo*), you don't know anything about the **television music channel**, so ask (*Laura*) some questions about it.

(Interlocutor shows question card 4D on page 99 to Pablo)

Use these words to help you. *(Interlocutor indicates prompt words)*

Do you understand?

Now *(Pablo)*, ask *(Laura)* your questions about the **television music channel**, and *(Laura)* you answer them.

4C

A great new TV channel:

MUSIC CHANNEL PLUS

starts 1 May

watch the latest music videos
and
listen to rock and hip-hop

visit **www.music.com** *for more information*

4D

Television music channel

- name / channel ?

- what kind / music ?

- date / start ?

- what / see ?

- website ?

Note: Candidates are assessed on both their questions and answers in Part 2 of the test.

Test 1 Key

Paper 1 Reading and Writing

Part 1

1 C   **2** E   **3** H   **4** D   **5** B

Part 2

6 A   **7** B   **8** C   **9** A   **10** B

Part 3

11 C   **12** A   **13** A   **14** B   **15** C
16 F   **17** C   **18** H   **19** A   **20** G

Part 4

21 B   **22** A   **23** C   **24** B   **25** A   **26** C   **27** B

Part 5

28 C   **29** A   **30** B   **31** B   **32** C   **33** C   **34** A   **35** B

Part 6
For questions 36–40, spelling must be correct.

36 face   **37** brush   **38** apple   **39** soap   **40** ambulance

Part 7
For questions 41–50, ignore capitals / absence of capitals. Spelling must be correct.

41 going / planning / hoping / preparing   **42** more   **43** like   **44** by   **45** of
46 and   **47** need / have   **48** eat   **49** if / because   **50** to

Part 8
For questions 51–55, spelling must be correct.

51 Best Bike Rides
52 Kim James
53 (the)12(th) / twelve / twelfth (of) April / 12/(0)4 / (0)4/12
54 39 West Road / Rd(.)
55 (£) 12.90 / twelve (pounds) (and) ninety (p/pence)

Sample answer A

Mark: 5

> Hi Jay,
> I left my blue bag in your house yesterday. In bag is my books and pencils.
> Please bring my bag to school. My bag is in kitchen on table. See you soon.
> Domingo

All three parts of the message are clearly communicated with only occasional grammatical errors.

Sample answer B

Mark: 4

> Dear Jay,
> Have you got my bag? I was left in the bedroom on the your bed. Bag is color
> blue. I have in my bag my things.
> Chu Hua

All three parts of the message are communicated with some non-impeding errors in spelling and grammar.

Sample answer C

Mark: 3

> Hi Jay,
> I leave my bag in your house? It is a blue colour. I leaved it in your room.
> Please bring to school on next Monday.
> Akram

Two parts of the message are clearly communicated (the response does not address what is inside the bag).

Sample answer D

Mark: 2

> Hi
> My like bag is leave for you house on table.
> I have got bag in make up and miwror
> Please you can bag?
> Thank you.
> Amadis

Only two parts of the message are communicated (the response does not address the colour of the bag). The errors in expression may require interpretation by the reader and impede communication.

Sample answer E

Mark: 1

> DEAR JAY – HAVE YOU GOT MY GREEN COLOUR BAG?

Only one part of the message is communicated.

Paper 2   Listening

Part 1
1 B   **2** A   **3** B   **4** C   **5** B

Part 2
6 C   **7** A   **8** E   **9** H   **10** G

Part 3
11 C   **12** B   **13** C   **14** A   **15** C

Part 4
For questions 16–20, ignore capitals / absence of capitals. Spelling must be correct.
16 Thursday / Thurs   **17** 5.15 (p.m.) / five fifteen / (a) quarter past five / 17.15
18 (by) bus   **19** (£) 4.50 (p/pence) / four pounds (and) fifty (p/pence)   **20** (a) jacket

Part 5
For questions 21–25, ignore capitals / absence of capitals. Spelling must be correct.
21 (0)7.45 (a.m.) / seven forty(-)five / (a) quarter to eight   **22** (fashion) show
23 (a) camera   **24** (£) 3.25 (p/pence) / three pounds (and) twenty(-)five (p/pence)
25 (the) 24(th) (of) June / twenty(-)fourth (of) June / 24.06 / (0)6.24

Transcript

This is the Cambridge Key English Test for Schools. Paper 2, Listening Test number 1. There are five parts to the test. Parts One, Two, Three, Four and Five. We will now stop for a moment before we start the test. Please ask any questions now because you must NOT speak during the test.

[pause]

PART 1 *Now, look at the instructions for Part One.*

[pause]

You will hear five short conversations. You will hear each conversation twice. There is one question for each conversation. For each question, choose the right answer, A, B or C.

Here is an example:
Which is the girl's horse?

Boy:	Is that your horse over there, with the white face?
Girl:	No. Mine is the one with two white legs. Isn't she pretty?
Boy:	Oh yes, standing next to the black one.
Girl:	That's right. Would you like to ride her?

[pause]

The answer is A.

Now we are ready to start. Look at question one.

[pause]

Question 1 *One. What's Sally doing now?*

Friend:	Hello, Mrs James. Is Sally at home? I want her to come and play tennis with me.
Mrs James:	Sorry, she isn't. She's gone for a walk across the fields.
Friend:	What time will she be back?
Mrs James:	In about an hour because she wants to go for a swim before dinner.

[pause]

Now listen again.

[repeat]

[pause]

Question 2 *Two. Where did the woman find the ball?*

Toby:	Can I have my ball back please, Mrs Salter? I kicked it over the wall by mistake!
Mrs Salter:	I can't see it in the flowers by the wall, Toby.
Toby:	It went in the tree, I think.
Mrs Salter:	I can't see it there. Oh look! It's on the path. Here! Catch!

[pause]

Now listen again.

[repeat]

[pause]

Question 3   *Three. How will Bella get to her friend's house this afternoon?*

Bella:	Can you drive me to my friend's house this afternoon? The one who lives on the farm.
Father:	Can't you cycle there, Bella? You don't get enough exercise.
Bella:	But it might rain, Dad, and it's too far to walk there.
Father:	Oh OK. But this is the last time.

[pause]

Now listen again.

[repeat]

[pause]

Question 4   *Four. What job does Mark's sister do?*

Friend:	I saw your older sister yesterday, Mark.
Mark:	Was she at the fashion show?
Friend:	No… at an art competition.
Mark:	Oh that's right. She had to take photos of the winning artists. That's her job.

[pause]

Now listen again.

[repeat]

[pause]

Question 5   *Five. What's the date of Adrian's birthday party?*

Girl:	Has Adrian invited you to his fourteenth birthday party? It's in July.
Boy:	Yes, he has. But it's in August, isn't it?
Girl:	Oh yes, sorry. On the third.
Boy:	That's right. It's the day after mine, but I'll be fifteen!

[pause]

Now listen again.

[repeat]

[pause]

That is the end of Part One.

[pause]

PART 2   *Now look at Part Two. Listen to Sam talking to a friend about his family.*
Which sport does each person do now?
For questions 6 to 10, write a letter A to H next to each person.
You will hear the conversation twice.

[pause]

Friend:	Sam, there are so many photos in your house of your family doing sport!
Sam:	Yes. This is my grandfather in a swimming competition in 1970. He's seventy-five now but he still swims.
Friend:	Wow!
Sam:	My dad was good at swimming too. But he's in a hockey team now and he does that instead.
Friend:	And who's this standing next to the boat in this picture?

Sam:	Hmm … My brother Chris. He went sailing once, but didn't like it. He's an excellent climber and spends every weekend doing that.
Friend:	And is this him too?
Sam:	No, that's my uncle Steve. He goes skiing three times a year. He loves sport. He's going to start sailing next year too.
Friend:	And what about your sister? She's in the school football team, isn't she?
Sam:	She does play for the school but for the volleyball team, not the football team.
Friend:	And your mum?
Sam:	She comes to watch all of us play, of course. She really likes watching dad play hockey. But she's actually a great tennis player. That's what she's doing right now.

[pause]

Now listen again.

[repeat]

[pause]

That is the end of Part Two.

[pause]

PART 3   *Now look at Part Three. Listen to Emma talking to a friend about her photography course.*
For each question, choose the right answer, A, B or C.
You will hear the conversation twice.
Look at questions 11 to 15 now. You have twenty seconds.

[pause]

Now listen to the conversation.

Friend:	Hello Emma. Are you doing a photography course?
Emma:	Yes. There wasn't one at my high school, Parkplace, so I go to Riverside School on West Road.
Friend:	Are your classes in the afternoon?
Emma:	Yes. I finish high school at two o'clock and get home at two-thirty. The classes begin at a quarter to three.
Friend:	Is it expensive?
Emma:	A twelve-week course is usually eighty pounds. But it costs me sixty-five pounds because I'm still at high school. There's also a six-week course for forty-five pounds.
Friend:	Do you enjoy the course?
Emma:	It's great. The cameras are quite old, but my photos are improving quickly so I'm pleased. But I'll never be a famous photographer.
Friend:	Is taking good photos hard?
Emma:	Well, we did people first, and they're not easy. But then we took pictures of flowers, which was much easier. We're going to photograph animals next.
Friend:	And after the course?
Emma:	I'm not ready for a competition yet, but I'd like to take more photos to show my friends. I can use my mum's digital camera for that.

[pause]

Now listen again.

[repeat]

[pause]

That is the end of Part Three.

[pause]

PART 4   *Now look at Part Four. You will hear a boy, Richard, talking to a friend about visiting the circus.*
Listen and complete each question.
You will hear the conversation twice.

[pause]

Richard:	Hi Claire. I'm going with my cousin to Zippo's circus next week. Do you want to come with us?
Claire:	What day, Richard?
Richard:	We wanted to go on Wednesday but there were no tickets left so we're going on Thursday afternoon instead.
Claire:	What time does the show start?
Richard:	At two-thirty and it ends at a quarter past five. We have to be home by six-thirty because my cousin has to go out that evening.
Claire:	How will we get there?
Richard:	There aren't any trains so we'll go by bus. It's too far to walk.
Claire:	OK. Are the tickets expensive? I've only got seven pounds.
Richard:	Oh, that's all right. They're only four pounds fifty each.
Claire:	Great! That leaves me with two pounds fifty to get some ice-cream or a drink. Is there anything I need to bring?
Richard:	You'll need a jacket because it's cold inside the circus tent. But don't bring your mobile. You don't want it to ring during the show.
Claire:	Great! I can't wait!

[pause]

Now listen again.

[repeat]

[pause]

That is the end of Part Four.

[pause]

PART 5   *Now look at Part Five. You will hear a teacher giving some information about a trip to a museum.*
Listen and complete each question.
You will hear the information twice.

[pause]

Teacher:	I'd like to tell you a few things about our school trip to the Fashion Museum later this month.
	We'll travel there by bus at seven forty-five a.m. so you have to be at school fifteen minutes earlier, at seven-thirty. You mustn't be late!
	When we get to the museum, there's time to look around in small groups. They've got lots of clothes from the nineteenth century and it's important you see those. And we'll meet again later to watch the museum's fashion show at two o'clock.
	You don't need to bring any sandwiches because there's a café there but you'll need a camera to take some photos for your school project.

Usually, tickets for the museum are five pounds seventy-five but we're getting a special group ticket so you only have to pay three pounds twenty-five. That's two pounds fifty less than usual.

If you're interested in going, you need to let me know soon. The trip's on the twenty-fourth of June so you need to pay by June the tenth.

[pause]

Now listen again.

[repeat]

[pause]

That is the end of Part Five.

You now have eight minutes to write your answers on the answer sheet.

Note: Teacher, stop the recording here and time eight minutes. Remind students when there is **one** minute remaining.

[pause]

That is the end of the test.

Test 2 Key

Paper 1   Reading and Writing

Part 1
1 F   **2** D   **3** C   **4** H   **5** E

Part 2
6 B   **7** A   **8** C   **9** A   **10** C

Part 3
11 A   **12** B   **13** C   **14** B   **15** C
16 F   **17** D   **18** A   **19** H   **20** B

Part 4
21 B   **22** A   **23** A   **24** C   **25** B   **26** B   **27** B

Part 5
28 B   **29** C   **30** A   **31** B   **32** A   **33** C   **34** B   **35** C

Part 6
For questions 36–40, spelling must be correct.

36 sofa   **37** clock   **38** plant   **39** light   **40** table

Part 7
For questions 41–50, ignore capitals / absence of capitals. Spelling must be correct.

41 are   **42** would   **43** going / planning / hoping / preparing   **44** next / this
45 of   **46** do   **47** to   **48** if   **49** or   **50** me

Part 8
For questions 51–55, spelling must be correct.

51 Aztec Gold
52 (the) 18(th) / eighteen(th) (of) June / 18/(0)6 / (0)6/18
53 (£)4(.00) / four (pounds)
54 (0)9.30 (a.m.) / half past nine / nine thirty (in the morning)
55 (at) (the) park (nearby)

Sample answer A

Mark: 5

> How are you?
> Yesterday my dad took me to the football studim in town. We watched
> football match Benfica v Braga. It was the best! We went home after 3 hours.
> Ana Maria

All three parts of the message are clearly communicated with only minor grammar and spelling errors.

Sample answer B

Mark: 4

> Hi Alex,
> Yesterday I went to sports stadium 'maracanã'. I was go with my dad. We
> was see the fotball and staying for all match 2 hours. We arrive in house at
> 7p.m.
> Write me soon,
> Paulo

All three parts of the message are communicated with some non-impeding errors in spelling and grammar.

Sample answer C

Mark: 3

> Hi Alex,
> Yesterday I went to watch football at the stadium with Carlos and Victor. It
> was great and we win! We are the best team!
> Your friend,
> Rafael

Two parts of the message are clearly communicated (the response does not address how long you stayed there).

Sample answer D

Mark: 2

> Dear Alex,
> This week we was match at stadum. I go because in intersing. I go with Toni.
> Franco make the goal. I love Footaball!

Only two parts of the message are communicated (the response does not address how long you stayed there). The errors in expression may require interpretation by the reader and impede communication.

Sample answer E

Mark: 1

> Hi Alix,
> How are you? On Monday I went to stadium and watched there football. I tell you how long you stayed there.
> Wrte me soon.
> Best wishes,
> José

Only one part of the message is communicated.

Paper 2   Listening

Part 1
1 C   **2** A   **3** A   **4** B   **5** C

Part 2
6 D   **7** A   **8** H   **9** G   **10** C

Part 3
11 B   **12** B   **13** C   **14** A   **15** B

Part 4
For questions 16–20, ignore capitals / absence of capitals. Spelling must be correct.
16 (0)8.30 / eight thirty / half past eight (a.m.)   **17** Crystal   **18** field
19 (£) 1.50 (p/pence) / one (pound) fifty (p/pence)   **20** 12 / twelve

Part 5
For questions 21–25, ignore capitals / absence of capitals. Spelling must be correct.
21 Tuesday / Tues   **22** silver   **23** (£) 160 / one/a hundred (and) sixty (pounds)
24 87 / eighty(-)seven (North Street)   **25** 5.45 / five forty(-)five (p.m.) / (a) quarter to six / 17.45

Transcript

This is the Cambridge Key English Test for Schools. Paper 2, Listening Test number 2. There are five parts to the test. Parts One, Two, Three, Four and Five. We will now stop for a moment before we start the test. Please ask any questions now because you must NOT speak during the test.

[pause]

PART 1   Now, look at the instructions for Part One.

[pause]

You will hear five short conversations. You will hear each conversation twice. There is one question for each conversation. For each question, choose the right answer, A, B or C.

Here is an example:
Which is the girl's horse?

Boy:	Is that your horse over there, with the white face?
Girl:	No. Mine is the one with two white legs. Isn't she pretty?
Boy:	Oh yes, standing next to the black one.
Girl:	That's right. Would you like to ride her?

[pause]

The answer is A.

Now we are ready to start. Look at question one.

[pause]

Question 1   One. Where is William's mobile?

William:	Have you seen my mobile, Mum? I left it on top of the fridge last night.
Mother:	I think it's on the table by the front door, William.
William:	That's yours, Mum!
Mother:	Oh… (laughs) Well, yours is in my coat pocket then! Sorry! I thought it was mine.

[pause]

Now listen again.

[repeat]

[pause]

Question 2   Two. How much is a ticket for today's match?

Friend:	Hey Julia! I'm going to the volleyball match now. Come with me!
Julia:	How much are the tickets?
Friend:	They're usually five pounds but because they've got so many left they're only two pounds fifty now. It'll be a great game.
Julia:	That's lucky. I've only got four pounds in my purse.

[pause]

Now listen again.

[repeat]

[pause]

Question 3   *Three. Which is the boy's sister?*

Boy:	Look, that's my sister over there, talking to her friends.
Girl:	Do you mean the girl with the blonde hair? She's pretty!
Boy:	My sister's got dark hair.
Girl:	Oh... I see her. And she's got your hat on!

[pause]

Now listen again.

[repeat]

[pause]

Question 4   *Four. Where will they meet?*

Boy:	I'll see you at the entrance to the stadium for tonight's concert, shall I?
Girl:	Why don't we meet at the bus stop instead, or even better, at the café? We can get something to eat there before the concert starts.
Boy:	But we have to collect our tickets from the stadium first.
Girl:	Oh, OK then.

[pause]

Now listen again.

[repeat]

[pause]

Question 5   *Five. What will they do this evening?*

Girl:	It's too hot to play table tennis this evening. Let's stay inside and watch that DVD instead... that one with Johnny Depp in.
Boy:	But it's Carol's party this evening. We're going to that, aren't we?
Girl:	Oh yes! I forgot. So let's watch that film tomorrow, OK?
Boy:	All right.

[pause]

Now listen again.

[repeat]

[pause]

That is the end of Part One.

[pause]

PART 2   *Now look at Part Two. Listen to Sophie talking to her mother about presents for the family. Which present will she buy for each person?*
For questions 6 to 10, write a letter A to H next to each person.
You will hear the conversation twice.

[pause]

Mother:	Here's the men's department, Sophie.
Sophie:	Great. I can get lots of my presents here. I'll get some socks for Nick.
Mother:	Oh look. Your dad would love this shirt.
Sophie:	But I bought him one last year.
Mother:	You can never have too many.
Sophie:	Oh, OK. What about this sweater for Uncle Tim?

Mother:	Mmm. He's got a lot of sweaters, a hat is better.
Sophie:	OK. What shall I get grandpa then? A pen?
Mother:	I think a watch is more useful.
Sophie:	You're right. He's always late for things. And Max? Those orange sweaters look good.
Mother:	But he prefers dark colours. This T-shirt is better and it's black.
Sophie:	Right, I'll get that. Now something really special for Ben. This jacket's beautiful.
Mother:	Don't be silly, Sophie. You can't buy him a leather jacket!
Sophie:	It's my money!
Mother:	What about this pen?
Sophie:	But he's already got so many.
Mother:	This one's special — he'll love it and it's much cheaper than the jacket.
Sophie:	Oh. All right then. I'll get that.

[pause]

Now listen again.

[repeat]

[pause]

That is the end of Part Two.

[pause]

PART 3   *Now look at Part Three. Listen to Jay talking to a friend about a holiday he went on with his family. For each question, choose the right answer, A, B or C. You will hear the conversation twice. Look at questions 11 to 15 now. You have twenty seconds.*

[pause]

Now listen to the conversation.

Girl:	Hello, Jay, did you get back from holiday on Friday or Saturday?
Jay:	Sunday.
Girl:	Where did you stay?
Jay:	My parents don't like city-centre hotels so we stayed in a hotel right on the beach. The mountains were twenty minutes away by car.
Girl:	Was there a pool?
Jay:	It was great! I swam in it every day. There were tennis courts as well but I'm no good at tennis. Of course my dad spent all day playing golf!
Girl:	Did you have your own room?
Jay:	My brother and I had one together. It was OK – there was a TV. But if we wanted to use a computer or get a drink from the fridge we had to go to our parents' room.
Girl:	What was the food like?
Jay:	It was fine. There was fish and lots of different salads every day but I prefer pasta so I nearly always had that.
Girl:	So was it a good holiday?
Jay:	My parents said the hotel was really comfortable and not too noisy. It wasn't expensive either, so we may go back again!

[pause]

Now listen again.

[repeat]

[pause]

That is the end of Part Three.

[pause]

PART 4   *Now look at Part Four. You will hear Maria talking to her teacher about a school hockey competition. Listen and complete each question.*
You will hear the conversation twice.

[pause]

Maria:	Hello, Mrs Walker.
Mrs Walker:	Hello, Maria. You haven't forgotten the hockey competition on Tuesday, have you?
Maria:	Oh, no. What time are we starting?
Mrs Walker:	We'll begin at nine but can you be here at half past eight? I've got a job for you.
Maria:	OK. What is it?
Mrs Walker:	I want you to meet the players from the High School when they get here. The teacher's name is Mr Crystal.
Maria:	Pardon?
Mrs Walker:	Crystal. C-R-Y-S-T-A-L. Meet their bus in the car park and take them all to the school field. They can wait there until the other teams arrive.
Maria:	OK, Mrs Walker. Will I need to bring any money with me?
Mrs Walker:	Well, you've already paid two pounds for the competition but you'll need one pound fifty for a snack. It'll be a long morning and everyone'll get hungry.
Maria:	Right. Are a lot of other schools going to be here?
Mrs Walker:	Two schools can't come but there will still be twelve playing in the competition. It should be a good day.
Maria:	Great! I hope we win!

[pause]

Now listen again.

[repeat]

[pause]

That is the end of Part Four.

[pause]

PART 5   *Now look at Part Five. You will hear a man leaving a message about a bike. Listen and complete each question. You will hear the information twice.*

[pause]

Man:	Hello, this is John from City Bike Shop. You asked us to get a bike from Holland for you. Well, it's going to arrive on Monday, but I have to check it, so you can come and get it on Tuesday. I know you wanted a red one, but they haven't got any in that colour. Sorry! So they're sending a silver one instead. Hope that's OK? I'm sure you'll love it.
	You'll be pleased because this bike is a bit cheaper. It was one hundred and eighty-five pounds, but now it's only one hundred and sixty. It's a good price for this kind of bike.
	Remember, don't come to the shop at thirty-three North Street. We're a hundred metres down the road at number eighty-seven, opposite the supermarket. We only repair bikes at number thirty-three.
	Please don't come at lunch time if possible. We're very busy then. We're open every day until five forty-five p.m. And I'm here every morning from eight-thirty.
	Well, that's all, I think… (fade)

[pause]

Now listen again.

[repeat]

[pause]

That is the end of Part Five.

You now have eight minutes to write your answers on the answer sheet.

Note: Teacher, stop the recording here and time eight minutes. Remind students when there is **one** minute remaining.

[pause]

That is the end of the test.

Test 3 Key

Paper 1 Reading and Writing

Part 1
1 H   **2** D   **3** A   **4** G   **5** E

Part 2
6 B   **7** C   **8** A   **9** B   **10** C

Part 3
11 A   **12** A   **13** C   **14** B   **15** B
16 E   **17** B   **18** H   **19** G   **20** A

Part 4
21 B   **22** A   **23** A   **24** C   **25** B   **26** C   **27** A

Part 5
28 A   **29** C   **30** A   **31** B   **32** C   **33** A   **34** B   **35** C

Part 6
For questions 36–40, spelling must be correct.

36 library   **37** restaurant   **38** factory   **39** museum   **40** supermarket

Part 7
For questions 41–50, ignore capitals / absence of capitals. Spelling must be correct.

41 and   **42** at   **43** are   **44** be / become   **45** do   **46** of
47 have / 've   **48** to   **49** for   **50** about

Part 8
For questions 51–55, spelling must be correct.

51 Fashion Show
52 bus
53 (the) 28(th) / twenty(-)eight(th) (of) Feb(ruary) / 28/(0)2 / (0)2/28
54 (£) 14(.00) / fourteen (pounds)
55 287229

Sample answer A

Mark: 5

> Hi Alex!
> I am very happy to hear that you are coming to my party. Is in my house and starts 6 p.m. – you can bring pizza, cola, chisps and DVDs. See you soon.
> Love,
> Andrea

All three parts of the message are clearly communicated with only minor spelling and grammatical errors.

Sample answer B

Mark: 4

> Dear Alex,
> How are you? I'm write because I want you say that party starts at 5 o'clock in my house. Please bring the good present. I Like CD.
> Marco

All three parts of the message are clearly communicated with some awkwardness of expression.

Sample answer C

Mark: 3

> DEAR ALEX,
> IT'S GREAT YOU WILL COME TO MY BIRTHDAY PARTY. COME AT 3 P.M. TO MY HOUSE. DALIBOR AND ROKO WILL COME TOO. WE WILL HAVE FUN. BYE AND SEE YOU SOON.
> MIRO

Two parts of the message are clearly communicated (the response does not address what to bring).

Sample answer D

Mark: 3

> Hi Alex,
> The party started at 5 o'clock in the afternoon. We stayed at my house and played a game. My uncle bring the best present Shakira CD. It was best birthday.
> See you soon,
> Maria

All three parts of the message are included but the context is incorrect.

Sample answer E

Mark: 0

> Dear Alex,
> I'd love to come to your party. What time does it start? Wher is? What do I bring?
> Gianfranco

The question has not been attempted.

Paper 2 Listening

Part 1

1 A   **2** C   **3** B   **4** C   **5** B

Part 2

6 H   **7** D   **8** F   **9** E   **10** B

Part 3

11 B   **12** A   **13** C   **14** B   **15** B

Part 4

For questions 16–20, ignore capitals / absence of capitals. Spelling must be correct.

16 Robbie   **17** 9.30 (a.m.) / half past nine / nine thirty

18 car   **19** swimming   **20** (a) snack

Part 5

For questions 21–25, ignore capitals / absence of capitals. Spelling must be correct.

21 8(th) (of) July / eighth (of) July / July eighth / (0)8.07 / (0)7.08   **22** (the) park

23 hip(-)hop   **24** 337140   **25** Monday

Transcript

This is the Cambridge Key English Test for Schools. Paper 2, Listening Test number 3. There are five parts to the test. Parts One, Two, Three, Four and Five. We will now stop for a moment before we start the test. Please ask any questions now because you must NOT speak during the test.

[pause]

PART 1   *Now, look at the instructions for Part One.*

[pause]

You will hear five short conversations. You will hear each conversation twice. There is one question for each conversation. For each question, choose the right answer, A, B or C.

Here is an example:
Which is the girl's horse?

Boy:	Is that your horse over there, with the white face?
Girl:	No. Mine is the one with two white legs. Isn't she pretty?
Boy:	Oh yes, standing next to the black one.
Girl:	That's right. Would you like to ride her?

[pause]

The answer is A.

Now we are ready to start. Look at question one.

[pause]

Question 1   *One. What doesn't the girl like about her photo?*

Girl 1:	Look at this photo of me at Clara's party. I hate it!
Girl 2:	What's wrong with it? Your dress looks beautiful.
Girl 1:	The dress is all right, but my shoes are terrible.
Girl 2:	But your hair looks lovely and the dress is great so what's the problem?

[pause]

Now listen again.

[repeat]

[pause]

Question 2   *Two. What will Tim do first?*

Mother:	Your room looks really untidy, Tim. You need to clean it.
Tim:	But I've got some important homework to do.
Mother:	OK, do that first and then do your room, and you can't watch TV until you've done both of those things.
Tim:	OK, Mum.

[pause]

Now listen again.

[repeat]

[pause]

Question 3   *Three. Which is the girl's next lesson?*

Girl:	Oh no... I've forgotten my history book.
Boy:	Is that your next class?
Girl:	In five minutes. Then I've got science just before lunch and art this afternoon.
Boy:	Here... take my book. But remember to give it back to me after school. See you later.

[pause]

Now listen again.

[repeat]

[pause]

Question 4   *Four. What is Sonia going to eat?*

Woman:	What would you like for dinner, Sonia?
Sonia:	Not chicken again. We're always having that. How about some fish instead?
Woman:	I haven't got any fish and it's too late to get any from the shop. But I've got some pizza. You always like that.
Sonia:	OK. That sounds good.

[pause]

Now listen again.

[repeat]

[pause]

Question 5   *Five. What did Jack's mum give him for his birthday?*

Girl:	Did you get that mobile phone for your birthday, Jack?
Jack:	It was my Christmas present. I got some money from my mum for my birthday.
Girl:	Oh great, what are you going to buy with that?
Jack:	I want to get a bike but I haven't got enough. I'll have to save for a few months.

[pause]

Now listen again.

[repeat]

[pause]

That is the end of Part One.

[pause]

PART 2   *Now look at Part Two. Listen to Lucy talking to a friend about a new sports centre.*
What is the problem with the different places at the sports centre?
For questions 6 to 10, write a letter A to H next to each place.
You will hear the conversation twice.

[pause]

Boy:	Have you been to the new sports centre yet, Lucy?
Lucy:	Well, I went swimming there on Saturday with my dad, but it was really crowded.
Boy:	So was it hard to get a space in the car park?
Lucy:	Yes, it's just not big enough.
Boy:	Hmm ... Did you visit the café?
Lucy:	We wanted some hot drinks but we didn't stay. The tables weren't very clean.

Boy:	That doesn't sound good. But the sports shop's OK, isn't it?
Lucy:	Not really. Everything there costs so much.
Boy:	But I hear they have a good dance club.
Lucy:	That's right. My sister wanted to go but it's too early in the evening for her. It's a pity because it's not expensive to join.
Boy:	Do they have any other clubs?
Lucy:	I went to the basketball club last week but it wasn't any fun – we didn't do much.
Boy:	But basketball's really exciting! You should watch one of the big teams play.

[pause]

Now listen again.

[repeat]

[pause]

That is the end of Part Two.

[pause]

PART 3 *Now look at Part Three. Listen to Simon talking to a friend about a school trip.*
For each question, choose the right answer, A, B or C.
You will hear the conversation twice.
Look at questions 11 to 15 now. You have twenty seconds.

[pause]

Now listen to the conversation.

Girl:	Hello, Simon. How was your school trip? Was it on Monday or Tuesday?
Simon:	Wednesday actually.
Girl:	What was it like?
Simon:	Really good! We visited a science museum, a motorbike factory and a TV centre. The motorbike factory was only open in the morning so we went there first. We saw the museum and the TV centre in the afternoon.
Girl:	Was the TV centre any good?
Simon:	We had to be quiet because they were filming and it was really hot standing near the lights. But it wasn't crowded – we were the only visitors there.
Girl:	Did you go shopping?
Simon:	Yes, after eating our sandwiches in the park. I just got a poster. The T-shirt I liked was too small.
Girl:	What about the museum?
Simon:	We looked at some boring old clocks first, but then a museum guide told us some interesting things about space travel. They also have some old musical instruments there but we didn't have time to see them.
Girl:	Did you take any photos?
Simon:	I took some of my friends before we had lunch in the park. We couldn't take any in the motorbike factory.

[pause]

Now listen again.

[repeat]

[pause]

That is the end of Part Three.

[pause]

PART 4 *Now look at Part Four. You will hear a girl speaking on the telephone.*
Listen and complete each question. You will hear the conversation twice.

[pause]

Robbie:	Hello, is Amy there?
Man:	Sorry, she's gone out. Can I take a message?
Robbie:	Yes, please. My name's Robbie.
Man:	How do you spell that?
Robbie:	R-O-B-B-I-E.
Man:	Right, I've got that.
Robbie:	It's about the shopping trip tomorrow. Can you tell Amy we're going at half past nine instead of a quarter to nine?
Man:	OK. I'll tell her.
Robbie:	And we're not going by train any more. My brother's going to drive us there in his car. He'll bring us back too.
Man:	Great.
Robbie:	He hates waiting so she must be ready!
Man:	OK. Anything else?
Robbie:	Yes! Tell her to bring her swimming things because there's a really good pool next to the shopping centre.
Man:	OK. I will.
Robbie:	And can you ask her to bring a snack – we won't have time to go to a café. But we can get a drink while we're walking around the shopping centre.
Man:	No problem. I'll let her know.
Robbie:	Thanks a lot. Bye.

[pause]

Now listen again.

[repeat]

[pause]

That is the end of Part Four.

[pause]

PART 5 *Now look at Part Five. You will hear a man talking on the radio about a competition to win concert tickets. Listen and complete each question. You will hear the information twice.*

[pause]

Man: Here's some great news for all our listeners. We have a special competition for you today and the first prize is two free tickets to see *Metro* in their big concert next month on the eighth of July. The tickets for their last concert on the fifteenth of April sold really quickly so it'll be difficult to get tickets this time. Their last concert was at the city stadium, but this is in the park so everyone will be able to enjoy the great summer weather.

Metro are quickly becoming very popular and they play great hip-hop music. To win tickets for their next concert all you have to do is answer this question: What's the name of their first CD? If you think you know the answer, the number to call is double-three, seven, one, four, oh.

Don't wait too long because the competition closes at five o'clock on Monday. We'll tell you the name of the winner in our programme on Tuesday.

Good luck everyone. And now back to some music.

[pause]

Now listen again.

[repeat]

[pause]

That is the end of Part Five.

You now have eight minutes to write your answers on the answer sheet.

Note: Teacher, stop the recording here and time eight minutes. Remind students when there is **one** minute remaining.

[pause]

That is the end of the test.

Test 4 Key

Paper 1 Reading and Writing

Part 1

1 F   **2** C   **3** H   **4** A   **5** D

Part 2

6 C   **7** B   **8** A   **9** B   **10** C

Part 3

11 C   **12** B   **13** B   **14** A   **15** C
16 G   **17** H   **18** A   **19** D   **20** E

Part 4

21 A   **22** C   **23** B   **24** B   **25** C   **26** A   **27** B

Part 5

28 C   **29** B   **30** A   **31** B   **32** A   **33** C   **34** B   **35** A

Part 6
For questions 36–40, spelling must be correct.

36 grass   **37** forest   **38** kite   **39** river   **40** mountain

Part 7
For questions 41–50, ignore capitals / absence of capitals. Spelling must be correct.

41 ago   **42** last / this / one   **43** are   **44** with   **45** the
46 lot / number / couple / school / shoal / group   **47** there   **48** more   **49** to   **50** of

Part 8
For questions 51–55, spelling must be correct.

51 (the) 29(th) / twenty(-)nine / twenty(-)ninth (of) July / 29/(0)7 / (0)7/29
52 (11) Market Street/St(.)
53 (£) 55(.00) / fifty(-)five (pounds)
54 (at)(the) library
55 (0)8.10 (a.m.) / eight ten / ten past eight (in the morning)

Sample answer A

Mark: 5

> Dear Robin
> I'm happy to hear you really like listening to music. I really like hip-hop and rock. I like Green Day and Metallica but best is Nirvana. I have got every CD's and DVD's
> Mali

All three parts of the message are clearly communicated with only occasional grammatical errors.

Sample answer B

Mark: 4

> HI ROBIN BEST MUSIC FOR ME IS HIP HOP. MY FAVOURITE BANDS IS YOUSSOUPHA, ROCÉ, AND MÉDINE LIKE. BUT MÉDINE IS MY MORE FOVOURITE. I HAD THE EVERY OF THEIR CD.

All three parts of the message are communicated with some awkwardness of expression.

Sample answer C

Mark: 3

> Dear Robin,
> How are you? I also like listening to music. I like rock and pop best. My favourite band is R.E.M. They Rock! Write me soon and tell me more.
> Igor

Two parts of the message are clearly communicated (the response does not address how many CDs) with only minor spelling errors.

Sample answer D

Mark: 2

> Hello Robin,
> Thank you for the email. I like listen music. Kind I like is. My favourite the
> Banditos. You like Banditos? The CD is I have all.
> Eve

Only two parts of the message are communicated (the response does not address the kind
of music). The errors in expression may require patience and interpretation by the reader and
impede communication.

Sample answer E

Mark: 0

> What kind of music do I like? Who is my favourite band? How many CD you
> have?

The question has not been attempted.

Paper 2   Listening

Part 1

1 A   **2** C   **3** B   **4** C   **5** A

Part 2

6 E   **7** F   **8** D   **9** B   **10** H

Part 3

11 B   **12** C   **13** B   **14** A   **15** C

Part 4
For questions 16–20, ignore capitals / absence of capitals. Spelling must be correct.

16 Friday   **17** (The) Ship   **18** (at) (the) station
19 7.30 (p.m.) / seven thirty / half past seven / 19.30
20 (£) 5.25 (p/pence) / five (pounds) (and) twenty(-)five (p/pence)

Part 5
For questions 21–25, ignore capitals / absence of capitals. Spelling must be correct.

21 Thursday / Thurs   **22** (£) 9 (.00) (p/pence) / nine (pounds)
23 (at) (the) (zoo) entrance   **24** (the) lions   **25** toys

Transcript

This is the Cambridge Key English Test for Schools. Paper 2, Listening Test number 4. There are five parts to the test. Parts One, Two, Three, Four and Five. We will now stop for a moment before we start the test. Please ask any questions now because you must NOT speak during the test.

[pause]

PART 1   *Now, look at the instructions for Part One.*

[pause]

You will hear five short conversations. You will hear each conversation twice. There is one question for each conversation. For each question, choose the right answer, A, B or C.

Here is an example:
Which is the girl's horse?

Boy:	Is that your horse over there, with the white face?
Girl:	No. Mine is the one with two white legs. Isn't she pretty?
Boy:	Oh yes, standing next to the black one.
Girl:	That's right. Would you like to ride her?

[pause]

The answer is A.

Now we are ready to start. Look at question one.

[pause]

Question 1   *One. What is Becky going to take for the picnic?*

Boy:	Hi Becky. Are you taking some cans of lemonade for the picnic?
Becky:	Of course, and a big pizza.
Boy:	I'm going to take a bottle of juice and some cakes.
Becky:	Chocolate ones, I hope.

[pause]

Now listen again.

[repeat]

[pause]

Question 2   *Two. How much is the mobile phone?*

Girl:	So which mobile phone are you buying with your birthday money, Joe?
Joe:	The *Vox 55*. It's lovely but I have to ask my parents for thirty pounds. It costs seventy-five.
Girl:	That's a lot of money. You could buy a lot of CDs for that!
Joe:	Well, mobiles are expensive.

[pause]

Now listen again.

[repeat]

[pause]

Question 3 *Three. Where will they buy the eggs?*

Girl:	I need some more eggs for my cake, Mum.
Mother:	OK. We can drive out to the farm and get some.
Girl:	It'll be easier to go to the shop down the road, or even the market.
Mother:	I know, but the eggs from there aren't as fresh. It won't take us long in the car.

[pause]

Now listen again.

[repeat]

[pause]

Question 4 *Four. What time does the film start?*

Girl:	Would you like to come to the film on Saturday, Ella?
Ella:	OK. What time?
Girl:	It begins at quarter to three but we have to get tickets, so let's meet at the cinema at quarter past two. It's a short film – only one and a half hours long.
Ella:	Good. We'll be home before five.

[pause]

Now listen again.

[repeat]

[pause]

Question 5 *Five. How will the boy travel to the beach?*

Girl:	My dad drove us to the beach yesterday. It was a great day out.
Boy:	Really, I'm going there tomorrow with some friends.
Girl:	Are you going by bus?
Boy:	It's the best way. The train station is such a long way from the beach.

[pause]

Now listen again.

[repeat]

[pause]

That is the end of Part One.

[pause]

PART 2 *Now look at Part Two. Listen to Rick and Helen talking about their friends and their favourite lessons. What is each person's favourite lesson?*
For questions 6 to 10, write a letter A to H next to each person.
You will hear the conversation twice.

[pause]

Rick:	Helen, we need to write about students' favourite lessons for the school magazine.
Helen:	OK, Rick. My favourite lesson is science, what's yours?
Rick:	Well, we have fun in art lessons but I'm no good at it. I do well in maths so I prefer that to everything else. What about Paul? Have you spoken to him?

Helen:	Yes – at first he couldn't decide between music and geography, but then he said he didn't like geography quite as much.
Rick:	Well, not many people like geography. Sunita said she really enjoyed history. She likes art too, but not as much. What about Robert?
Helen:	I know he's more interested in English than any other subject, but I couldn't talk to him because he's away at a music competition.
Rick:	Holly said her best subject is Spanish. She's interested in science too, but doesn't enjoy the lessons as much, because she doesn't like the teacher.
Helen:	Oh, really? I think she's nice. Now, what about the…

[pause]

Now listen again.

[repeat]

[pause]

That is the end of Part Two.

[pause]

PART 3 *Now look at Part Three. Listen to Joe talking to his mother about his day at school.*
For each question, choose the right answer, A, B or C.
You will hear the conversation twice.
Look at questions 11 to 15 now. You have twenty seconds.

[pause]

Now listen to the conversation.

Joe:	Hi Mum!
Mother:	Joe! You're home late. It's four o'clock!
Joe:	The bus was fifteen minutes late. We only left at a quarter to four.
Mother:	How was school today?
Joe:	Football practice was great. We used the sports hall, because it was too wet to play on the school field or in the park.
Mother:	Do your football clothes need washing?
Joe:	My shorts are fine, but the T-shirt's dirty and the socks too.
Mother:	Give them to me then. Is your next match soon?
Joe:	Yes. It was on the eighteenth of March, but they've changed it to the fifteenth. Oh, and I have to pay the teacher by the twelfth.
Mother:	More money! I've already given you four pounds fifty.
Joe:	That was just for the bus. I also want to get the photo of my team and that's two pounds twenty-five.
Mother:	OK. But that's six pounds seventy-five for everything. It's quite a lot!
Joe:	Not really, Mum. Anyhow, can I go and do my homework now?
Mother:	You've got history to do, haven't you?
Joe:	I did that yesterday. But I have to do maths homework by tomorrow.
Mother:	What about science?
Joe:	That's OK. That's next week.

[pause]

Now listen again.

[repeat]

[pause]

That is the end of Part Three.

[pause]

PART 4   *Now look at Part Four. You will hear a girl, Lucy, talking to a friend about visiting the cinema. Listen and complete each question.*
You will hear the conversation twice.

[pause]

Lucy:	Hi Jake.
Jake:	Hi Lucy.
Lucy:	I'm going with Cass and Alex to the Star Cinema this week. Would you like to come too?
Jake:	When are you going? I've got a lot of homework to do Thursday, so I have to stay in then.
Lucy:	We're going on Friday so that's OK.
Jake:	Which films are showing, do you know?
Lucy:	Well, we've missed a film called *Lucky Days*, which I wanted to see, but another one called *The Ship* is on this week. It's meant to be good.
Jake:	Great. Where shall I meet you?
Lucy:	Well, I've agreed to wait for everyone at the station and then we'll all go to a café before the film.
Jake:	OK. What time?
Lucy:	The film starts at seven thirty so we're going to meet at six o'clock. That'll give us enough time.
Jake:	And how much are the tickets? I hope they're not expensive.
Lucy:	They're seven pounds fifty full price but we'll get them for five pounds twenty-five – that's the student price.
Jake:	Great. See you later then.

[pause]

Now listen again.

[repeat]

[pause]

That is the end of Part Four.

[pause]

PART 5   *Now look at Part Five. You will hear a teacher talking about a trip to the zoo.*
Listen and complete each question. You will hear the information twice.

[pause]

Teacher: Before our trip to Westpark Zoo, I'd like you to write something for homework about a wild animal. Our trip is on Thursday, so I would like the homework on Wednesday.

The trip is nine pounds and if you haven't paid already, you must bring your money to school tomorrow. If you want to bring some money to spend you can, but not more than five pounds.

We get to the zoo at about eleven o'clock. Later on, we're going on a special tour with a zoo guide so everyone needs to be at the entrance at twelve-thirty for the start of that. The guide will then take us to the zoo's information centre before taking us to the insect house.

Now, remember you mustn't feed the zoo animals but of course you can watch staff giving them something to eat. The lions get their food at three o'clock and the elephants are given theirs at four.

There's a zoo shop and there'll be time to go there before we leave. You can buy postcards and toys there if you want. There's also a café where you can get some snacks.

[pause]

Now listen again.

[repeat]

[pause]

That is the end of Part Five.

You now have eight minutes to write your answers on the answer sheet.

Note: Teacher, stop the recording here and time eight minutes. Remind students when there is **one** minute remaining.

[pause]

That is the end of the test.

UNIVERSITY *of* **CAMBRIDGE**
ESOL Examinations

S A M P L E

Candidate Name
If not already printed, write name
in CAPITALS and complete the
Candidate No. grid (in pencil).

Candidate Signature ....

Examination Title

Centre

Supervisor:

If the candidate is ABSENT or has WITHDRAWN shade here ▭

Centre No.

Candidate No.

Examination
Details

0	0	0	0
1	1	1	1
2	2	2	2
3	3	3	3
4	4	4	4
5	5	5	5
6	6	6	6
7	7	7	7
8	8	8	8
9	9	9	9

KET Paper 1 Reading and Writing Candidate Answer Sheet

Instructions

Use a PENCIL (B or HB).
Rub out any answer you want to change with an eraser.

For **Parts 1, 2, 3, 4** and **5**:
Mark ONE letter for each question.
For example, if you think **C** is the right answer to the
question, mark your answer sheet like this:

Part 1

1	A B C D E F G H
2	A B C D E F G H
3	A B C D E F G H
4	A B C D E F G H
5	A B C D E F G H

Part 2

6	A B C
7	A B C
8	A B C
9	A B C
10	A B C

Part 3

11	A B C
12	A B C
13	A B C
14	A B C
15	A B C

16	A B C D E F G H
17	A B C D E F G H
18	A B C D E F G H
19	A B C D E F G H
20	A B C D E F G H

Part 4

21	A B C
22	A B C
23	A B C
24	A B C
25	A B C
26	A B C
27	A B C

Part 5

28	A B C
29	A B C
30	A B C
31	A B C
32	A B C
33	A B C
34	A B C
35	A B C

**Turn over for
Parts 6 - 9** →

Sample answer sheet - Reading and Writing (Sheet 2)

For **Parts 6, 7 and 8:**

Write your answers in the spaces next to the numbers (36 to 55) like this:

Part 6		Do not write here
36		1 36 0
37		1 37 0
38		1 38 0
39		1 39 0
40		1 40 0

Part 7		Do not write here
41		1 41 0
42		1 42 0
43		1 43 0
44		1 44 0
45		1 45 0
46		1 46 0
47		1 47 0
48		1 48 0
49		1 49 0
50		1 50 0

Part 8		Do not write here
51		1 51 0
52		1 52 0
53		1 53 0
54		1 54 0
55		1 55 0

Part 9 (Question 56): Write your answer below.

Do not write below (Examiner use only)					
0	1	2	3	4	5

Sample answer sheet - Listening

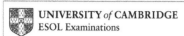
UNIVERSITY *of* **CAMBRIDGE**
ESOL Examinations

S A M P L E

Candidate Name
If not already printed, write name
in CAPITALS and complete the
Candidate No. grid (in pencil).

Candidate Signature

Examination Title

Centre

Centre No.

Candidate No.

Examination
Details

0	0	0	0
1	1	1	1
2	2	2	2
3	3	3	3
4	4	4	4
5	5	5	5
6	6	6	6
7	7	7	7
8	8	8	8
9	9	9	9

Supervisor:

If the candidate is ABSENT or has WITHDRAWN shade here ▭

KET Paper 2 Listening Candidate Answer Sheet

Instructions

Use a PENCIL (B or HB).

Rub out any answer you want to change with an eraser.

For **Parts 1, 2** and **3**:
Mark ONE letter for each question.
For example, if you think **C** is the right answer to the
question, mark your answer sheet like this:

0	A B C

Part 1

1	A B C
2	A B C
3	A B C
4	A B C
5	A B C

Part 2

6	A B C D E F G H
7	A B C D E F G H
8	A B C D E F G H
9	A B C D E F G H
10	A B C D E F G H

Part 3

11	A B C
12	A B C
13	A B C
14	A B C
15	A B C

For **Parts 4** and **5**:
Write your answers in the spaces next to the
numbers (16 to 25) like this:

0	example

Part 4		Do not write here
16		1 16 0
17		1 17 0
18		1 18 0
19		1 19 0
20		1 20 0

Part 5		Do not write here
21		1 21 0
22		1 22 0
23		1 23 0
24		1 24 0
25		1 25 0